MW00635941

WHAT DID WE GET OURSELVES INTO?

STORIES BY
FOREST SERVICE WIVES

NORTHERN ROCKY MOUNTAIN RETIREES ASSOCIATION
P.O. BOX 20186
MISSOULA, MONTANA 59801

WHAT DID WE GET OURSELVES INTO?

STORIES BY FOREST SERVICE WIVES

Copyright 2000 by the Northern Rocky Mountain
Retirees Association, Inc. (NRMRA)

Published in the United States of America

ISBN 0-912299-99-1

Publishing Consultant: Stoneydale Press Publishing Company,
Stevensville, Montana.

ALL RIGHTS RESERVED

No part of this book may be reproduced in any manner without the
express written consent of the publisher, except in the case of brief
excerpts in critical reviews and articles.

All inquiries should be addressed to:
Northern Rocky Mountain Retirees Association, Inc.
P. O. Box 21086
Missoula, Montana 59801

INTRODUCTION

In October 1944, then Regional Forester Evan W. Kelley penned the introduction to the first of the volumes, "Early Days in the Forest Service." Through collecting and publishing the tales of personal experiences, as told by the men who lived them, Regional Forester Kelley intended to record and preserve the human side of Forest Service history. Most if not all of those stories involve the exploits of the men who were hired to serve, protect and nurture the National Forests.

But there is another, equally fascinating side to compliment the adventures of the men of the Forest Service. That side is exposed through the stories told by the women who accompanied their men, for better or for worse, richer or poorer, in sickness or health to make homes, often literally in the wilderness, and provide strength, support, comfort and aid.

Almost to a person, when asked to provide a tale illustrative of some of their experiences, these women would reply, "I don't know what to write. We didn't do anything very special." Yet some weeks later we would find a letter in the mail and once again be amazed at the stamina, courage, humor and good sense that was once again revealed to us by these women who did nothing special.

The stories contained in this volume continue an effort begun by Forest Service wives living in the Washington, D.C., area some years ago, and so help to round out some of the anecdotal history of the Forest Service.

Here on the following pages are their stories.

James H. Freeman, President
Northern Rocky Mountain Retirees Association
Victor, Montana
May, 2000

FOREWORD

Forest Service wives of yesterday are a unique bunch of gals. We come from the city, small towns, farms and ranches, and our backgrounds are varied. But we all have one thing in common, we love our husbands who are part of the Forest Service family.

Every wife has a story to tell – reporting to a new job, or a transfer and moving, waiting for your husband to come home from a fire or detail, shared holidays, friendships that were made – the stories go on and on.

If we don't write our stories, no on will know what our life was like being "married" to the Forest Service. We lived in remote places with husbands gone for long periods of time, many of us didn't have the modern conveniences of indoor plumbing or electricity, and our children learned the importance of a family. Not a one of us would trade jobs!

EDITOR'S NOTE

The Northern Rocky Mountain Retirees Association (NRMRA) is the host for the 3rd National Forest Service Reunion planned for September 4th, 2000. What better time to explore the possibilities for a session on "the way we were."

Letters were sent to many Forest Service wives from Region 1, asking them to write a story. Through constant reminders, we came up with the following stories. (Then we had to go back and ask for pictures.)

Thank you so very much for writing a story! For those of you who missed the first opportunity, be a part of the next volume.

Thanks again, and enjoy your stories.

Note: All pictures accompanying our stories were provided by the authors, unless otherwise noted.

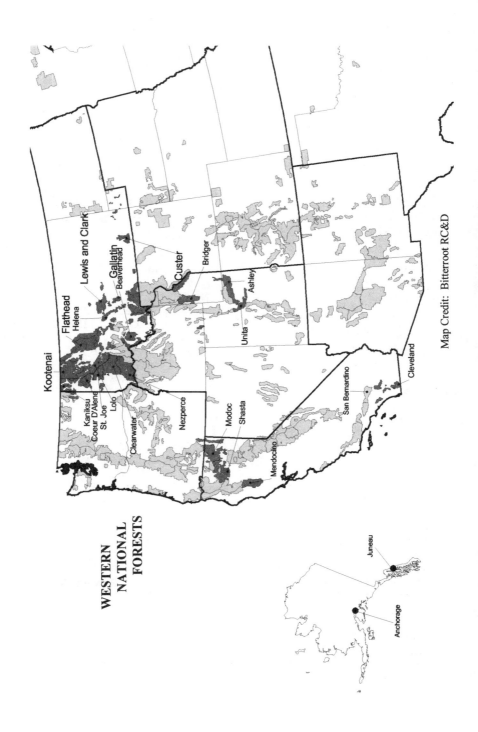

WESTERN NATIONAL FORESTS

Kootenai

Flathead

Lewis and Clark

Gallatin
Beaverhead

Helena

Custer

Bridger

Ashley

Unita

Kaniksu
Coeur D'Alene
St. Joe

Lolo

Clearwater

Nezperce

Modoc

Shasta

Mendocino

San Bernardino

Cleveland

Juneau

Anchorage

Map Credit: Bitterroot RC&D

vi

Alaska
  Anchorage
  Juneau
Idaho
  Clearwater N. F.
    Orofino
    Powell R.S.
  Coeur d'Alene N. F.
    Magee R.S.
    Kingston R.D.
    Shoshone Work Station
      (Wallace R.D.)
  Kaniksu N. F.
    Bonners Ferry
  Nezperce N. F.
    Cedar Flats Job Corps Ctr.
    Cottonwood Job Corps Ctr.
    Fenn R.S.
    Grangeville
    Moose Creek R.S.
    Slate Creek R.S.
  St. Joe N. F.
    Avery
    Calder
    Clarkia R.D.
    Princeton R.S.
    St. Maries
    Red Ives R.S.
Montana
  Beaverhead N. F.
    Lyons R.S.
    (old Madison N. F.)
  Bitterroot N. F.
    Hamilton
  Custer N. F.
    Dickinson Job Corps Ctr.
    Red Lodge
    Fort Howes R.S.
  Deer Lodge N. F.
    Anaconda Job Corps Ctr.
    Whitehall
  Flathead N. F.
    Big Prairie R.S.
  Gallatin N. F.
    Hebgen R.D.
      Quake Lake
  Helena N. F.
    Canyon Ferry
    Lincoln
    Townsend

California
  Cleveland N. F.
    Descanso R.D.
  Mendocino N. F.
    Willows R.D.
  Modoc N. F.
    Alturas
  San Bernadino N. F.
    Big Bear R.S.
    San Bernadino
  Shasta-Trinity N. F.
    Redding
    Hayfork
Utah
  Ashley N. F.
    Whiterock R.D.
    Roosevelt
    Vernal
  Uinta N. F.
    Heber R.D.
    Provo
Washington
  Colville N. F.
    Sullivan Lake R.S.
Wyoming
  Bridger N. F.
    Kemmerer

  Lewis & Clark N. F.
    Great Falls
  Lolo N. F.
    Plains R.D.
    Seeley Lake R.D.
    Superior
  Kaniksu N. F.
    Noxon R.S.
  Kootenai N. F.
    Eureka R.S.
    Fisher River R.D.
    Libby
    Rexford R.D.
    Sylvanite R.D.
    Yaak

Vigilante Range Experiment Station
abt. 40 miles so. of Sheridan MT

Dedicated to the wives of the men
of the United States Forest Service.

TABLE OF CONTENTS

ANNIVERSARY
about Doris Joy
as told by Dick Joy

This story involves my parents, Chic (C.A.) and Doris Joy, when they were stationed at the old Lyon Ranger Station on the West Fork of the Madison River, Madison N.F., Montana.

It was June 20th, 1926, their second wedding anniversary, and Dad was out in the field leaving Mother alone at the Ranger Station. K.D. Flock was working range surveys on the Forest and came by the station. Mother was despondent and over coffee K.D. finally got her to tell him why. K.D. then told Mom that if she could find a clean pair of Chic's pants and a shirt he'd take her to dinner. She produced, K.D. took a bath in the washtub behind the cabin, and donning her husband's clothes, took Doris to a nearby dude ranch for her anniversary dinner!

Mother often delighted in telling this story just to kid Dad. The highlight for me was when K. D. Flock told me the same story in 1991 at the first F.S. Retirees Reunion at Glenwood Springs, Colorado – some 65 years after the event. Unfortunately, all three parties have now passed on.

The old Lyon Ranger Station on the West Fork of the Madison River (found off U.S. Hwy. 287 south of Ennis, Montana, near the West Fork Rest Area).

ANOTHER SHORT STORY
about Doris Joy

In the 1920's, Rangers used horses more then vehicles. They would also hire saddle and pack stock from ranchers when Forest Service stock was unavailable. Such was the case when Doris took Chic Joy out to a distant ranch in their Model T Coupe so he could rent horses and ride range allotments on the old Madison National Forest. It was the fall of 1926 and Doris was pregnant with her first child. On the return trip in late afternoon she had a flat tire. As she was struggling to change it she saw a dust cloud coming down the road. Fearing gypsies that were reported to be in the area, she hurriedly unlaced one of her high-top boots and put her diamond wedding ring in the toe, then laced back up. She got her .22 caliber rifle out and stood it against the car for a show of force! The party arrived, being Mormons that were headed for Yellowstone National Park and had taken the wrong road. Seeing her condition, and in exchange for directions, they changed her tire and saw her on her way. Doris said it was one of the few times she really got scared being alone on a Ranger District. *(This story was told when they were living at the old Lyon Ranger Station.)*

Doris and C.A. "Chic" Joy.

EXPERIENCES OF A FOREST SERVICE WIFE
by Betty Robe (Mrs. Harvey O. Robe)

Harve and I were married June 1, 1932, in the fire season and at the bottom of the Great Depression. We spent our honeymoon at Big Bear Ranger Station, San Bernardino National Forest, California. My introduction to what a Forest Service wife should do and be was swift and amazing. In a few days I became fire dispatcher, smokechaser, office clerk, first aid nurse, as well as receptionist and caretaker when the men were in the field.

A loud banging on the door brought us out of bed about 11 p.m. our sixth night. I learned what Search and Rescue meant as a very distraught man at the door insisted we find his fishing companion (a woman whom we later learned was someone else's wife). They became separated on Holcomb Creek; when it became dark, he panicked and had a hard time getting back to his parked car. Harve assembled the District crew. They planned to go into the fishing area from intersecting trails, up and down Holcomb and north and south, with all to meet where Hanna Flats trail crossed the creek. Harve asked me to go along with the first aid kit; he carried blankets and rope in a big knapsack. We searched Hanna Flats trails, and arrived last at the meeting spot where we rested and talked about what to do next. Coxy Patrolman Vern Moon (a crusty, New Mexico ex-cowboy) said, "I wonder where the blank blank hell that heifer can be?" From a large patch of willow nearby came, "YOOHOO, HERE I AM!" Thus ended my first lesson on how really dedicated F.S. people were to public service.

The toughest frustration of my 34 years as a Forest Service wife was a very obnoxious chemical toilet in our ranger station bathroom. By agreement the State Health Dept. and the F.S. to protect domestic water supply all 580 homes on Government property had to have these chemical "splashers." Ours was especially splash-burn prone because a limestone ridge under the cabin prevented sinking the tank down a safe distance. I hated this situation, so as often as possible I'd drive or ride Nellie over to friends' homes in the resort community of Pine Knot.

Nellie was a gentle, beautiful bay mare. Mentioning her leads to memories of other events. The lush meadow pasture at our ranger station had not been grazed for years, and needed moderate use. When a saddle horse rental operator asked to use it, he was issued a permit for three horses he claimed were "too good to be rented to dudes." The horses turned out to be Nellie, a rodeo bucking bronco on which none of us wanted to try our luck, and a big, strong, black and white pinto circus mule, who had a torrid love affair with Nellie. Every time I rode out of the yard on her, he would let out loud brays and, on a dead run, sail over the pasture fence. This fool mule attracted a lot of public interest wherever we went, never leaving us until we returned to the ranger station.

One day Harve decided to pack trail signs with posts attached back to Sugarloaf Mountain country. I watched with horror the weird mule noises accompanied by near-miss biting, pawing and kicking activities. After about three hours, Harve decided there were easier ways to get those trail signs out. You can be sure I learned a number of words new to me during this hassle (which the mule won).

In the old days, few F.S. wives escaped the joy of packing water from springs, creeks or wells. I had taken water for granted when it came from city faucets, but lugging in gallons needed for cooking, bathing, laundry, etc., is some-thing else. A year later, CCC project #1 was a dandy, adequate pressure water system for our station. Hopefully, all other water-carrying wives were as fortunate.

Often I'd go with Harve on field trips. This was encouraged as a public relations activity. Sometimes I could be directly helpful, like the day we noticed a big pile of garbage and trash had been dumped in the parking lot at Bear Valley dam. Summer home people were suppose to dig garbage pits, but some persisted in decorating roadsides under cover of darkness, and were difficult to catch. While loading this mess for a trip to the real dump, we pawed through it and hit a jackpot – an empty pint whiskey bottle with a doctor's prescription label issued to a person we learned was a Los Angeles police captain, who was cited to appear in Judge Lind's Pine Knot Justice Court. He pleaded "Not Guilty," but both Harve and I testified. The Judge was a staunch F.S. cooperator. For cases involving illegal camp fires, smoking or fish and game violations, he frequently would ask Harve's advice on what the fine should be. Not in this case. The Judge said $500, maximum fine under the law. This, plus public watchfulness, has put an end to most such dumping.

We struck out, however, on night operations of timber sale cordwood permits. Policy was that only dead or down pine and fir trees could be sold by the F.S. Drought, bark beetles, etc., did not kill huge old yellow pine fast enough to suit several cordwood merchants. They would pick out an ailing tree, dig a trench around the base, and fill it with rock salt. The result was faster death to meet the strong demand for cordwood, which in those days was the only fuel available. Sadly, we were never able to get the goods on these tree bandits.

A stressful time for me was when we were separated for 12 days while Harve was on the infamous 219,000 acres Majilla fire on the Santa Barbara National Forest. It was toughest, though, when he rode "moonshine patrol" with back country mounted guard Vern Moon. Those years, prohibition under the Volstead Act was in full swing. It brought a lot of moonshine stills and boot-leggers to the north side of Big Bear District. Nearly every short creek or spring draining into the Mojave Desert had one or more whiskey pots on it. Fire risk was high, especially when gale force Santa Ana winds put flames into Bear and Holcomb Valleys in a hurry. F.S. policy was wise, I believe, to follow a friendly, cooperative approach, rather than trying to oust these lawbreakers. Also, little help could be expected from prohibition agents, who had bigger fish to fry. Yet it was a tense situation: two years before, the Coxy F.S. patrolman, Frank Hoopa was shot out of his saddle and killed by a tough still operator at Oak Spring, who falsely claimed that Frank had squealed on him. All this gave me the jitters, contrary to my usual "F.S. wife" state of mind.

Oh yes, we had bear problems too! But unlike Betty Cloninger's hilarious and productive bear experiences (imagine getting a bear rug and then bear-trapping a goodly supply of jerky and yummie canned venison to boot) – my story is sad. The California Fish and Game Department foolishly tried to bring back a long-gone bear population to Bear Valley country. Eight garbage-nuisance bears were live-trapped from National Parks and planted in several national forest areas. All were short lived. As ranger station office clerk, I handled many complaints because people seemed to think the F.S. was responsible. Even a beekeeper down near front country Highland was hopping mad, claiming bears had wrecked his bee hives. Near our Station a pack of dogs put a bear on top of a high tension powerline with fatal results. Civilization was simply too much for the poor bruins.

Most rewarding of events during my first year as a F.S. wife were my efforts to be "house mother" to 300 men down on their luck due to the 1929 stock market crash and its many negative ramifications, one of which caused thousands of men to drift to Southern California to search for a job, get away from freezing winter and try to salvage shattered lives.

With so many homeless, hungry, despondent people barely existing (most critical in the Los Angeles area). In early October 1932 the State came up with funds for soup kitchens, shelter and emergency medical care. For able-bodied men, work project camps were established. The F.S.

helped out by operating a number of these. Due to winter weather the only suitable facility was Camp Radford, an LA Recreation Department summer camp near our Converse Guard Station in the Santa Ana River basin. This setup was ideal, with a large central mess hall, kitchen, office, rec room, staff bedrooms etc., encircled by cabins with a capacity of 300 plus persons. Except for winter blankets, medical supplies and a few other items, all camp gear was on hand, including a caretaker who was a great help to my husband. The only problem was that no funds were available for camp and work project staff except for one assistant to Harve. Most of the so-called "bums" were happy and grateful for the good food, shelter and opportunity to work; yet there were a few rabble rousers and malcontent trouble makers. Three incidents I vividly recall:

1. One early December a medium strength earthquake hit. Most men were finishing dinner in the mess hall and the rest were in the rec room. I was waiting in our car so I could take Harve home to the Converse G.S. nearby, when suddenly, windows in both 1st and 2nd floors erupted with men bailing out of the large central building onto the hard ground below. Panic prevailed! My six years' experience as nurse for a doctor who made house calls was mighty helpful in caring for broken legs, ankles, concussions, shock, etc. Thanks of the injured men and camp doctors were sincerely appreciated.

2. A few days before Christmas, Butch, the camp meatcutter, broke into a summer home owner's wine cellar. There was no scarcity of willing hands to help pack containers full of "Dago red" to a cache near the camp. Merry-makers prevailed, and bad blood between some of them was spilled. To put a damper on all this, Harve turned out all lights and announced that the camp would be closed with no transportation out unless all the wine was turned in to the office. With the help of police, enough of the juice of the grape was turned in so that lights went back on. A situation loaded with dangerous potential was cooled off.

3. In late January a storm brought about 3 feet of snow. During the storm an elderly inmate passed on. At once several malcontents and trouble-makers started rumors the man froze to death or died of malnutrition and poor medical care. To quell the rabble rousers, near midnight, Harve and a husky assistant lashed the body to a toboggan and pulled it to Seven Oaks Resort where they were given bed and breakfast. A week earlier, my Redlands doctor had urged I go there to spend the rest of the winter there with my folks because I was carrying our baby and wanted no complications. The camp had phoned to tell me what took place there, and shortly after the storm put the phone lines out. Hearing

nothing further about the toboggan pullers, I went to the San Bernardino supervisor's office. I asked Supervisor Joe Elliott if he had had any word about Harve, and his answer was "No." I said if he was not going out to find the overdue party, I would go. This produced loud laughter from Assistant Supervisor John Everitt (a fine F.S. old-timer who as Supervisor, Shasta National Forest, lost his life while scouting a fast-moving forest fire). I guess the above scene (I was badly out of shape) gave John reason for his outburst, but I was serious!

Supervisor Elliott, good as his word, met the toboggan pullers about a quarter mile below end of snow cleared road at Camp Angeles. After loading the body in Joe's car, they all enjoyed a "snort" from his "emergency" brandy carried in his sheepskin coat. The coroner in San Bernardino said natural causes were responsible for the death.

This experience and others involving Forest Supervisor Joe Elliott made me realize why he was considered the Number One in the California Region. Joe said the Forest Service was his God. Much of his character, ideals and dedication rubbed off on people who worked for and with him. Joe was an inspiring leader, typical of F.S. old-timers.

In late March 1933, Harve was detailed to the Supervisor's Office to head up the Forest's work relief programs – Civilian Work Administration, CCC, WPA, ERA and NIRA – which helped pull our nation out of the Great Depression and gave the national forests many badly needed improvements.

We moved to San Bernardino and rented a furnished apartment. I was happy and relaxed, thinking the first exciting year as a F.S. wife was to end calmly. But not so!!

Unknown to us, we had moved next door to a paper currency counterfeiting outfit – four men and two women. Apparently they realized we heard their loud voices, noise of the printing machine, etc. That led to a warning from their tough looking leader. Meeting me on the sidewalk one day, he looked me up and down and said, "You want to have your baby, don't you?" I said "Yes" and he replied, "OK, you don't know nothing about us." Well, after some reflection, I tried to reach my husband by phone but he was in the field. So, on my own, I phoned the police. Within an hour police and U.S. Treasury Agents surrounded the apartment house and arrested all six counterfeiters without a shot being fired.

You can be sure I was very glad to return to Big Bear R.S. June 4th, to start typing work project plans for the three 200 boy CCC camps the District soon received. Thus ended my unforgettable first year as a

Forest Service wife.

SHISSLER PEAK LOOKOUT
by Julia Smith

My first experience with the Forest Service was in late summer in the early 1940's. De graduated from college in May and as we were newly married we needed some income, so De took a job as a lookout in the Bitterroot Forest – no place for a wife. I took a summer job in a church camp in Connecticut.

De wrote in late August that I would be permitted to join him on the lookout in September but I was to pack only the SMALLEST of bags. De's job was in the Moose Creek District, located in the Selway-Bitterroot Wilderness Area. The ranger station was not on any road. In fact it was 28 miles to the nearest road and food and personnel had to be either flown or packed in.

I was born in the West, but raised in the East, so this was a great adventure for me. I took the train to Missoula and there I was to contact the Johnson Flying Service for transportation to Moose Creek. I found I was listed as cargo in a Travel-Air 6000!

On my first plane ride I was determined to show how unruffled I was so I took out my knitting (four needle socks) and was doing just fine in the co-pilot's seat until it came time to land. Suddenly I'm looking at the ground, then the sky, then we seemed to be climbing the side of a mountain! First one needle came out then two, then three, so much for my cool.

The Ranger Station was right out of a book or a Western movie. I was astounded at the height of the trees with the log buildings looking so small underneath, the finishing touch being the newly killed venison hanging from the beams, it did feel to me like I was on a movie set. I soon found that they had no accommodations for an extra woman, so we were quickly put on horses and started out for Shissler Peak L. O. with the dispatcher as our packer. Now I understood the limited luggage. Getting the horse in a mood to climb after grazing the airstrip all summer proved beyond my equestrian experience so I started pulling her up the trail. De and the dispatcher noticed (finally) that I was missing and I got a lecture on how to make the horse behave – well the horse had other ideas so I ended up pulling her up the mountain.

When De saw what was happening we swapped horses. The dispatcher and I went on and De fell further and further behind. When the dispatcher and I arrived at the lookout it was clear that I would have to put together a meal. There was the typical tiny wood stove – at least I knew something about wood stoves – but then the dispatcher put a large hunk of elk out and it was beyond my limited cooking abilities – so we made a deal for him to cook the elk and I would cook the rest.

About an hour after we had arrived De showed up with the reins over his shoulder pulling the horse up the trail. He wasn't any better than I was at keeping her moving.

I soon discovered the limitations of high altitude lookout cooking. I knew we had to eat meals from what was on hand. One of the things on hand was 15 cans of sauerkraut, obviously not a choice of previous lookouts. I had no kitchen skills worth much and had to rely on a cookbook created by the regional office. Some of the recipes were truly delicious, but many things that a beginner ought to know were omitted. I avoided the bread problem as long as possible with muffins, biscuits, corn bread, etc., but soon realized that if we were not to become airborne I would have to bake some bread. The recipe for bread took 2 days, you started the evening before and by morning the bread would have risen and be ready to shape and raise one more time before baking. It didn't quite work out that way, but I finally made something that passed as bread.

All water was packed to the lookout in canvas bags, a five gallon back pack and two 2 gallon hand bags. My first day being fresh from the city I volunteered to get the water. I put on the back pack and picked up the two hand bags and with a hop skip and jump I was at the water hole. I filled the three bags and learned lesson number one about uphill and downhill with filled water bags. Sliding down was easy – going up (or trying to) resulted in more sliding down. There were no trees or bushes to help the upward steep, crumbly ascent. I had forgotten the mile high altitude, the three tenths of a mile stretched to five miles. Red in the face and exhausted I fell down and yelled to De for help. His first comment was, "you are losing water!" I was scolded for not pouring out some of the water (who's kidding – it was like GOLD.)

Fire Season that year lasted until late October. We did handle some small smoke chaser fires, and puzzled the R.S. with our "yell phone." They couldn't understand how I could tell them how the fire mopping up was going when the fire was more than a mile away by trail.

It snowed on October 20th and we were ordered down from the lookout. We hated to leave. We hiked down to the R.S. and the female problem was with us again. Ranger Gunderson finally offered us the use of his bath facilities. I was in the shower washing my hair and was told the plane to return us to Missoula had landed and we were to leave NOW, no time to finish the shower. Wet hair and all we climbed on the plane and returned to Missoula.

I don't know what Gunderson thought of our abilities to double up in a small space with a single cot, but I wondered afterwards if my stay had any influence on the subsequent decision that it was possible to have women lookouts.

Note: Yell phone instructions:

Cup hands megaphone style

Face receiving station

Yell one word (not more than two syllables)

Count mentally, one onethousand, two onethousand

Yell second word

and so forth

Works great on fairly still days or with the wind

Shissler Look Out
Moose Creek R. D. Nezperce N. F.

HONEYMOON
by Betty Cloninger

Russ Cloninger graduated from Forestry School at the University of Idaho in 1941. He immediately went back to work for the Forest Service at Red Ives Ranger Station on the St. Joe National Forest.

He had been working there every summer since he was fifteen years old. Times were tough in the 30's. And since he was of the big kind, he lied about his age in order to get a job. You didn't have to prove your age in those days. So every year when he filled out his Form 57, he wrote down 18 years old. After the third year, Supervisor Ray Fitting, asked, "Waddy, when are you ever going to be eighteen?"

Russ and I had met at the University of Idaho and had immediately fallen in love. We were prepared to get married as soon as his first paycheck arrived. In 1941, when you worked for the government, you had to work a month and then wait another month for your first check to arrive. On August 1, it finally arrived. It was for $83. Russ called me in Boise and jubilantly exclaimed, "Now, we can get married."

He informed the ranger that he was going out to get married. "Out" was 40 miles down the St. Joe River from Red Ives Ranger Station to Avery, Idaho; then 60 miles down the river to St. Maries; then 100 miles to Lewiston, Idaho, and Clarkston, Washington.

"You can't go, it's fire season," exclaimed Ranger Joe Frykman. But go he did, and luckily he still had a job when he got back.

My folks loaded all my worldly goods into a homemade trailer and drove with me from Boise to Lewiston. The trailer also contained a new $30 daveno to sleep on in our tent. I had put $5 down and the promise of $5 a month until paid off.

I had been preparing all summer. Girl friends had given me a bridal shower, I had gathered dish towels and scatter rugs to furnish our 14 x 16 tent. We met Russ and his folks in Clarkston, Washington, where they lived. With the help of two sets of parents, we had a nice church wedding and reception on the lawn.

Our $83 bought us one night in a motel, and the second night sleeping on the ground in the woods. The old trailer behind the 1937 Ford coupe held the daveno, a month's supply of groceries, a new broom, and a $2 bottle of Jack Rose whiskey for the "shivaree." We had 25 cents left when we got to the tent.

While sleeping out on the ground, Russ wakened in alarm. He thought he was having a heart attack, because he could feel a wild thumping in his chest. Oh no, I could feel a thumping in my chest, too. Turned out to be an old grouse drumming on a log nearby. The sound was traveling through the ground to where we were lying. Guess it was grouse mating season, too.

Yes, we did have a "shivaree." While we were away they had hung horse bells up in the corners of our tent. Then strung telephone wire out in the woods so they could ring the bells at the proper time. Boys came from the trail crew, the cook shack, a few lookouts, the horse packer and his wife, and the Ranger and his wife. They waited until dark, and then "all hell broke loose." Horse bells ringing over our heads, gunshots outside, wild Indian yells. The packer beat a hole in the new washpan with a stick. Joyous celebration! We invited them all inside our tent, opened up the bottle of Jack Rose whiskey and passed it around. Everybody tipped it up and had a slug! No, Russ didn't lose his job.

That was a memorable first summer. We lived in our 14x 16 foot tent on a wooden frame. The packer and his wife lived in another tent about 50 feet away. We carried water from Red Ives Creek nearby, and I kept a milk crate submerged in the creek for refrigeration.

The packer's wife, bless her heart, let me wash our clothes in her "kick-start" gasoline washing machine. The boys carried water from the creek for us, and we heated one tub full in a copper wash boiler on a lookout cook stove.

A big old black bear raided our camp almost every night. He took several bullets from our shoot-em up midnight bear fights. We finally got him in a bear trap that fall and made a rug out of him.

That bear trap provided another exciting episode. At day-light one morning, while Russ was away on a trip, there came a frantic knocking on my tent door. "Betty, Betty, get up, get up!" "We got a deer in the bear trap and we have to butcher." It was the packer from next door, and not yet deer season. But you can't let good meat go to waste, especially when you only get a supply truck from town once a week and you have no refrigeration to keep meat.

So we hustled the deer into the packer's tent, and the three of us skinned and cut up the deer, filled the canning jars with meat and started them processing in the copper wash boiler.

Boiling water bath for canning meat takes 3 or 4 hours of continuous boiling. The packer got rid of the "evidence," and we were pretty proud of our morning's work in saving all that good meat.

Along in the afternoon we were busily stoking the fire in the little lookout cook stove. There was a roast in the oven, and the wash boiler was merrily boiling away. To our consternation, here came the ranger's wife walking up the trail to "come calling." "My goodness, what are you boiling, it smells so good." The packer's wife just waved her hand airily and said, "Oh, we are just boiling the dish towels to make them white." Then we all sat down for a cup of tea!

What a bunch of renegades we were in our youth!

THE WHITEHALL PARADE
by Mabelle Hardy

In June, 1941 as a bride I joined my husband in Whitehall, Montana, where Mike was to spend the summer as assistant ranger. His job there related principally to range management. Grazing was not his specialty. According to the ranger, his job was to inspect range, keep records and empty "spittoons." Soon after we were settled in our tiny revamped lean-to-house Mike was sent out to spend three days inspecting range. To qualify for the job he had been required to provide his own car. Thus, an ancient Model A coupe, a huge horse trailer; and a good sized

"Working out to be a ranger's wife".

—13—

horse accompanied Mike on the safari.

The evening he was expected to return we planned to meet the evening east-bound and meet an elderly dowager friend during her train's brief pause in Whitehall. The purpose of the date was to introduce my brand new husband to her. But he did not get home by train time. To keep the date with this imperious little lady I went myself to the station. She was there on the vestibule between cars, and she was a very deaf lady. I greeted her and apologized for Mike's absence in loud, ringing tones as follows: "I'm sorry Mike is not here. He has been gone for three days and I'm not sure where he is and don't know when he'll be home." I'm sure this was audible to a few of the local folks and established our position in the community.

Later I prepared a welcome dinner for Mike and sat listening for his car to come in the yard. Time got later and later and at last I heard the clop, clop of horse's hooves. The little Model A had given up the ghost several miles out of town. Mike had just solved the problem by parking the car and trailer on the road shoulder and goaded the old hard-mouthed government Morgan horse in to town and dinner. The next day we drove my elegant Dodge coupe out and I towed the entourage back through Whitehall's main street.

So much for honeymooning on the Whitehall range.

CHANGE and MOVING
by Betty Cron

The first Sunday I was at Syracuse University was the luckiest day of my life. As one of three stragglers from my freshman cottage going on an Outing Club hike, we found three fellows from the College of Forestry along the way, waiting to escort us in the right direction! And so I met the love of my life, Bob Cron. Bob was in love with Forestry, I fell in love with him, and we were married three years later, and started our life on the San Bernardino National Forest. That was a big move for me, having been born in New York City, and my friends thought that going so far west meant I would have to live in a tent amongst the Indians!

Little did I realize that we would be moving often – and I remember that from the time he could talk young Bob would frequently ask, "When we gonna move, Mommie?" He seemed to like it, and I guess it was good training for his career in the F.S. later on!

At first transfers occurred about every two years – and three times it involved moving our cow, Nellie – and it was just a matter of getting a moving company and getting the job done. I always hated to leave wherever we were, but loved it the minute we got settled in the new place. Had to get used to living without electricity at Baron Flats, cooked on a wood stove, ironed uniform shirts with sad-irons, and made do with Coleman lanterns and a burlap covered cooler with water dripping on it, on the back porch. But I never had to live in a tent – though I got used to one for camping.

I think about the fifth move we made was to Willows, California, on the Mendocino. Bob went there first and came back with the news that he thought we should buy the house of a forester who was being transferred, and we were sort of committed to it, though I hadn't even seen it, since we had two little boys and needed a place to come to. It was a nice little 3 bedroom house, but the bathroom, which was between the two back bedrooms, had the bathtub and wash basin in it, and the toilet was in its own little room in a corner of a screened porch off the kitchen. That did have some advantages, but was a most unusual arrangement!

We lived there for two years, until one evening as we were coming out from a P.T.A. meeting, the Forest Supervisor's wife and I met in the hall, and she put her arms around me and said, "Oh, Betty, we're so sorry to lose you." I was dumb-founded and just hugged her back, and Bob and I went out the door and walked home in silence until I finally asked him where we were going, since Nona said she hated to lose me!

It turned out to be Alturas, California, on the Modoc, which was known in the Forest Service as Little Siberia, complete with Iron Curtain. That move involved selling the house, and then moving two little boys who had the measles at a very inopportune time. I don't remember the significance of the Iron Curtain, but I can recall walking to work one winter when the temperature was 32 below zero and the air sparkled like diamonds!

We lived there for ten years – in two different houses at the Forest Service warehouse compound – and each time a transfer came up (as I later learned) Bob would say that his wife wouldn't go, or that we wanted the boys to finish high school there, for he dearly loved the work and the people there – as well as the great duck and goose hunting up at Tule Lake!

But in February of 1958 Bob came home with a F.S. publication that gave the game census on all the National Forests. He had apparently been studying it because a transfer to Libby, Montana, as supervisor of the

Kootenai was in the wind. I could tell that the counts of the big game in Montana was really exciting him. But he also thought I might not want to give up my job in the D.A's office and leave California. (I'm so glad we did), and although Bob was already in college at Oregon State, Larry was still in high school.

But I said I thought if he was every going to take a forest, it ought to be that one, with all those game animals. But that was a big move with a lot more than usual involved. We made a trip up to Missoula (where he learned he didn't have much choice but to take the job, as his successor on the Modoc had already been selected) and we went on to Libby to look for housing. But housing was scarce and we decided to buy some lots, and that I would stay in Alturas until Larry graduated from high school, and Bob would move up and stay in a rooming house where Kenny Larson was living. Meanwhile I would work on house plans and see if I could work out something with a builder in Libby.

As luck would have it, Bruce Path was being transferred from the Kootenai. Bob called to tell me, and wanted to know if I thought we should buy his house. As we had visited with Bruce and Naomi when I was in Libby, I knew the house and liked it so we decided that was the best thing to do, and later sold the lots. So Bob settled in to the new job, and back to Alturas for Larry's graduation, and we made the best move of our lives by coming to Montana.

It was also the biggest – after ten years accumulation – and the hardest, for it was tough to pull up stakes and move so far from country we knew. But I loved it the minute we got settled, for I was now "retired" after nine and a half years as a working wife (by choice and in my prime) and I learned to "coffee", play bridge, golf, and ski – what a great life! And we lived in our nice home in Mt. View across the river from Libby for six years, until the move to Missoula came up. NOTHING is as certain as CHANGE!

But we did make the move – after much house hunting, and spending a month at the Shady Rest Motel until the house was ready. And for almost two years I felt it was the toughest move (for me) that we had ever made. I had really loved Libby – and my goodness, that was the first home we had with a furnace and a thermostat! But the real problem was that Missoula was TOO BIG. Little did I know in 1964 how it was going to grow.

Now, after 36 years here, I feel almost like a native – at least an 'old-timer' (in more ways then one!) And I know that our move to Missoula was a good one, and I am especially happy that Larry and Nancy moved here from Libby when he retired a few years ago, as it is the first time one of our sons had lived in the same town since they were in college.

So, at long last, we realize that – though we often resisted it, there were also lots of good things about MOVING! You can't let the grass grow under your feet.

A RANGER'S DAUGHTER
by Betty Parsell Gauld

When my Dad, Jack Parsell, came home from the Army after WW I, he went to work for the Forest Service as a seasonal employee. The forestry school at MSU (now UM) offered a short course which he attended, he took the ranger exam and was appointed ranger at Moose Creek, in 1921. He was in charge of building a ranger station. The building is still there, but is now used for something else.

He and Mom (Julia Hartman) was married that year and in the spring of 1922 they rode horses to Moose Creek. Dad said that she was scared to death the whole way – and it is a long way on a horse – or on foot. There were no bridges then so the streams, which were high in the spring, had to be forded.

The next year I was born, in 1924 Polly arrived and in 1925 Andy was born. From 1923 to 1925 Dad was on the Middlefork District and we all went there to live. I think the Middlefork District was what we called Number One Station and Pete King. Things were pretty primitive and Mom said one of my first comments as we came into the "dwelling" was, "Dirty house!"

In 1926 Dad was on the Bear Creek District, which was way out in the wilderness and because it would have been very difficult to move 2 toddlers and a baby on horseback to the station, we did not move up there with him. He was away from home weeks at a time. Mom told me that I told him when he came home that I had two Daddies. He was alarmed and asked, "Where is your other Daddy?" I told him that he was on top of the piano – his picture. She said that as she was pushing Polly in the buggy down town in Kooskia where they lived, Polly would ask every time they passed a man, "Is that my Daddy?"

Living separated this way wasn't easy so Dad decided to buy a farm and he quit the Forest Service and bought 60 cows and a bull and they had a dairy. He really hated that, so he went back to work for the Forest Service and Mom's brothers and cousins helped with the dairy and farm work until the dairy was sold. We continued to live on the farm and again Dad was gone a lot.

In the summers we would meet Dad wherever he was working for picnics – at places like 3 Devils, Cool Water and the Selway Falls. It is still very beautiful in those places. Once we went to a place up the Van Camp Hill where Dad had a crew of CCC boys planting trees. The road up there was very narrow, steep and scary. It isn't used anymore. We didn't have a car as Mom couldn't drive so we had to depend on relatives and friends to take us to meet Dad, but I think they enjoyed these outings too.

In the winter in the 1930's Dad had 2-man crews in the Lochsa, Selway, and South Fork of the Clearwater, and the Salmon for a wildlife study and he snowshoed alone from crew to crew to gather their information. He said he logged 1300 miles one winter on snowshoes. I'm sure Mom must have worried about him as there was no communication. We kids were used to his being gone. When he came home, it was a very happy occasion – and interesting too, as he had all sorts of bugs and worms in vials. The crew would operate on the animals which had died in the winter to discover the cause of death, and he would bring these things back for study.

In 1938 he was transferred to Grangeville as forest dispatcher and Dad was home most of the time. That was a happy time for us.

In 1941 Dad took leave of absence from the Forest Service to work for the Montana State Fish and Game Department and we moved to Missoula. He traveled all the time and Mom was along again. I had left to go to Spokane to business college, Polly went into nurses' training in Helena, Andy joined the Navy and Mom was alone with David, 10 years old, and Phyllis, 1 year old. She was unhappy so Dad returned to the Forest Service and after a short time in Sandpoint, he was appointed ranger of the Moose Creek District again.

Now they could travel to the ranger station by plane and Mom could be with Dad at Moose Creek when school was not in session in the summers. He worked in the supervisor's office from November to April. David and Phyllis grew up at Moose Creek and Phyllis has written the following story about their lives during that time.

MOOSE CREEK DAYS
1945 - 1955
by Phyllis Parsell Wolfinbarger

Early Years

Jack Parsell and Julia Hartman were married On December 18, 1921 in Elk River, Idaho. That spring of June 1922 Dad and Mom took off for their honeymoon to Moose Creek. Dad went ahead of Mom with the pack string and Mom followed behind with her horse. The creeks and rivers were high at that time of year and they had to ford the high creeks. Mom was really frightened, but she just hung on to her horse and followed along. Dad set up headquarters at Moose Creek and built the first log building that had an office in the front part and a cookhouse in the back part. It was a log structure of 30 x 40 feet. It had hardwood floors, a huge wood cook stove, big deep sinks and log tables with benches to feed large crews.

Mother remembered someone telling her that someday there would be a highway through there. Well, that never happened, but an airport was built in 1931 by mule power. Dad left Moose Creek and had ranger districts in other areas like Pete King and Number One. In 1941 Dad took a leave of absence from the Forest Service to do big game study for Montana Fish and Game. That is when we moved to Missoula I was a baby and my sister Betty (Susan) started at the University. Dad did this

Ranger Jack Parsell standing beside the cook-house and office building built in 1921.

study until 1944 and we moved to Sandpoint, Idaho for a brief time. In 1945 Dad was asked if he wanted Moose Creek back again. Yes, of course! So Mom, Dad, David and myself who was 4 years old moved to Hamilton, Montana. Moose Creek was at that time on the Bitterroot National Forest. In 1921 it was on the NezPerce. Moose Creek is now back on the NezPerce Forest. Moose Creek was absorbed into the Fenn Ranger district in 1995.

Moose Creek 1945

Mom and Dad packed up our clothes, lots of food, cleaning supplies, toys, etc. to last the summer. We all got on the old Ford Tri-Motor for the big trip over the Bitterroots into the Selway Wilderness. The old Ford Tri-Motor was used for Smoke Jumping, hauling freight and such. The plane was loaded with crates of oranges, apples, canned goods and whatever they needed at the Ranger Station. We would find a spot to sit down on a crate of oranges or cantaloupes and try to get comfortable for the next 45 minutes. We took off from Hamilton airport early one June morning. I hung onto Mom's pant leg because I was a little nervous riding in the big plane that was so full of heavy cargo. Mom was nervous too. She really didn't care about flying over those rugged mountains.

Mrs. Fred Parks was there to greet us and invited us to the cook house for lunch while our belongings were taken to the Ranger's house. There was an old wagon pulled by two mules named Skinny and Caboose. The wagon was loaded with all the supplies from the plane to the commissary. Mrs. Parks was the cook there at that time.

My brother David loved to scout around in the woods. One day he ran into a mother bear and he thought she would run from him. Well, she didn't. Mom said "David you look kind of pale." I guess he never tried that again.

It was a busy summer. Pack strings coming and going, fires and Smoke Jumpers around. Our house did have a bathroom and running water. The wood cook stove in the kitchen heated our water. We had a huge bath tub in the bathroom. It was brought in on skids pulled by a mule up the river. The house was really quite cute. It was log and had hardwood floors, and a wood floor furnace that was in a full basement. It had two bedrooms, one on the main floor and one upstairs where the bathroom was. It had no electricity in it. That meant no light, electric range, refrigerator or water heater. On hot days that wood cook stove really heated up the house so Mom tried to do all her cooking for the day in the morning before it got too hot. Some foods like butter or eggs were

Ford Tri-motor.   *JHF photo.*

kept in a cupboard in the basement. We had the spring that we kept some things in. I remember cases of Coca Cola were kept in the spring. Coca Cola was in bottles at that time. Fresh milk was something we didn't have. There was no way we could keep it. There was canned milk or powdered milk.

Washing clothes was quite a job. Mom had two big wash tubs she would set on two benches on the back porch. She carried the water from the kitchen faucet to fill her tubs. She put soap in one tub and the other tub was for rinse. She used an old wash board and a plunger to clean the clothes. Then rinsed them in the rinse tub and wrung them out by hand and hung them out to dry. They had a big old laundry type washing machine that was gas powered. It was like a huge barrel with holes in it that went around one way and stop and then go the other way. Dad would run that sometimes for her so she could wash blankets and large things. After the washing was all hung on the line to dry Mom would gather the clothes off the line. She would iron most all the clothes with an old heavy iron that was heated on the wood cook stove. There was a cook named Nola Holt who had a gas iron. It had a little gas tank below the handle and you could light it and it would iron clothes just like an electric one. But mother was afraid of gas, so she preferred the old fashioned way of ironing. In those days there was no such thing as permanent press.

August came and Mom was busy packing our things for the plane trip back to Hamilton. David was in school then and we had to leave the mountains so he could attend school. We usually left around the 20th. Dad had to stay until November 1. The station was then locked up until the next spring. Dad and his crew usually flew in around April 15.

Moose Creek 1946

Mother had bought an old oak dropleaf table and buffet for our log cabin. It was flown in by the Ford Tri-Motor. It is still there today.

Dad would set up a pup tent for me to play in. We always had a mother cat and kittens. I played with those kittens all summer. He also made me a swing. Later he made another swing so that when other children came they had a swing too. I was never allowed around the horses or mules. "Mules had a tendency to try and kick your head off." My parents were very careful that I did not get hurt. If you were hurt you were a long ways from a doctor or hospital. An airplane could not always get in there to get you out right away.

We had rattlesnakes to watch out for too. One day Mom noticed a kitten looking and backing up and looking and backing up. She stepped out on the back porch and saw a huge rattlesnake coiled up ready to strike at some kittens. She hollered out for Dad. She got no response, so she stepped to the old crank telephone and called him. He answered the call and came and shot the snake. Every June Dad would be gone about two weeks to put the telephone line up to Lost Horse cabin. Every winter snow would blow it down and so every spring Dad and another person would put the line back up. At that time Hamilton had telephone operators and you could crank up the phone at the office in Moose Creek and call out to Hamilton. The station had a switchboard that would connect us with the outside world. You had to talk really loud in order to be heard.

Right off the airport down in the trees there was a shelter for campers. It was made of logs and the front end of it was open. We used to walk down to the shelter and build a fire in the big fire ring and roast canned hot dogs. That may sound strange, but fresh meat was something we didn't have much of. No refrigeration, no meat. We ate canned chicken, Tuna fish, canned beef stew, canned hot dogs and of course Spam. I love Spam today. My kids think I'm crazy; they hate it. The commissary did have bacon and ham. I guess we had bacon too. I just don't remember it. Mom always canned elk meat and brought that with her too.

We always had the summer bear. Moose Creek would not be Moose Creek without the summer bear. One evening it was getting dark and Dad was gone out on the trail somewhere. I looked out the window and noticed a big black bear running around the outside of the corral. "Mom!" I said, "call George Wright, I just saw a big black bear go around the corral." "Oh sure you did," Mom said, "Now go to bed." Soon we heard a gun shot. Sure enough, the biggest bear you ever saw. He was about to get into the warehouse. He was not a grizzly, in fact we never saw a grizzly the whole time we were in there. I think there might have been a few, but we never saw them around the ranger station at all. We always went down to the shelter after a camper left to see what the camper left. Well, a bear beat us there. Mom picked up a stick and a piece of cardboard and banged it together and ran the bear off. He was eating something in the fire ring that the camper left.

Springtime

One spring after school was out in early June, Mom said, "Let's surprise Dad and just show up." So, Mom made arrangements with the Forest Service to fly us in. Well, we arrived and Dad was real surprised and happy to see us. Except, he was having Guard School in the living room of our cabin! Well, that's okay. Mom stayed in the kitchen and out of the way during class time. Dad had put a long table in the living room for the men. I made myself at home and sat down with them and went to class too. One morning Dad built a training fire for the men to fight fire. It was a wet spring and his fire wouldn't burn. He was really disappointed. I said, "Dad, why don't you put some gasoline on that brush?" "I'll bet it will burn then." Well, Dad took my advise. Sure enough, it took off and those men really had to keep ahead of it. That fire took place where a campground is today. Dad said that was the best training fire he ever had.

We didn't always fly in the Ford Tri-Motor. Sometimes we flew in the orange and black Travel Air. It wasn't as big as the Tri-Motor. It only had one engine where as the Tri-Motor had three engines. I remember Bob Johnson flying us in sometimes and Bob Vallance flying us in. I remember Bob Vallance giving me chewing gum. It would help to keep your ears from plugging up at high altitudes. I remember we flew out on the Tri-Motor with the door off and with a bunch of Smoke Jumpers. There seemed to be turbulence that day. We hit rough air and Mom let a yell out of her and grabbed a smoke jumper. I can still see them Smoke Jumpers laughing.

Fresh produce would not keep very long if it was brought in by the plane. Fresh oranges, apples, grapefruit and cantaloupe would keep good in the dark cook commissary. But for fresh vegetables, we grew them in the huge garden. The garden had an eight foot high pole fence around it. That kept the deer and elk out. We raised, peas, carrots, potatoes, lettuce, tomatoes, corn, cabbage and onions. We also had a great strawberry patch and a large raspberry patch as well. I loved the berries. Mom and Dad always ate theirs with sugar and canned milk. I liked mine right off the bush. Dirt and all. In the lower part of the garden they raised alfalfa and oats for the mules. Watermelon was a real treat. We never got watermelon unless someone brought it in to us. When someone brought us a watermelon we would invite others around the station and we had a feast. Sometimes people would bring in ice cream packed in dry ice. Boy, what a treat that was! Everyone would gather at the cook house and we would all feast together.

Julia Parsell in the raspberry patch beside the cookhouse and office building.

Our house had a large front porch and in the evenings we would set out on the porch and watch the elk or deer graze on the air strip. In the spring the cow elk would have their calves in the forest off the airstrip. In the evenings they would bring their little ones out to eat. I would try and get as close to them as possible. I would get close enough to almost touch them.

We always tried to make at least one trip to Moose Creek Ranches. Moose Creek Ranches was four miles up Moose Creek. They were lucky, they had a cow, electricity and cement sidewalks. They had their own airport as well. We either walked or rode horses. The ranch is now gone.

We didn't have a lot of entertainment back at Moose Creek, so we made up our own. Dad liked to fish in the evenings, so Mom would pack a lunch and we would go down to the river and eat lunch on the river bank. There was one favorite spot we went to a lot. It was called the point. It was where Moose Creek and the Selway Rivers came together. The beach was sandy and we could build a fire and Dad could fish and we could wade in the cold water. Sometimes we would cook the fish for supper over the fire. In early summer the Mock Orange was in bloom along the River and Mom and I would pick a fresh bouquet to bring home. In July there was thimbleberries and huckleberries. In late spring there was all kinds of beautiful wild flowers in bloom. It was the most beautiful place in the world. Dark rich ferns blanketed the forest floor with huge White Pine, Ponderosa Pine, Grand fir, and Lodgepole Pine. It was very quite. No car noises, dogs barking or people yelling. Only the sounds of birds and the wind blowing through the trees. Occasionally we had the sound of an airplane landing or taking off or flying over the ranger station. I hope it always remains wilderness. However, I hope it remains accessible to people. So they can enjoy the peace and quiet and reflect. Everyone needs to get away from the hurried lifestyles, the computers, the telephone and get back to nature and feel refreshed.

Moose Creek 1954

In 1954 modernization was coming to Moose Creek. The cookhouse was getting a propane refrigerator. Everyone was excited. That wasn't all we were getting. The station was getting a tractor. Old Skinny and Caboose were not needed for haying or pulling the wagon anymore. We had a tractor! Johnson's Flying Service flew in the refrigerator and the tractor. The next summer Mom had an old Maytag wringer type washing machine converted to gas and had it flown in on the Tri-Motor. She also had an old electric refrigerator converted to gas and flown in. Life was getting easier for Mom. The Travel-Air or Tri-Motor flew in about every two weeks with our mail and groceries. We always looked forward to having the plane come in. Now we could have fresh milk part of the time. Our garden produce would keep and we could order more perishables. Mom could make Jello too!

Our groceries were ordered by radio or telephone out to the Supervisor's office and then someone did the shopping for us. Our groceries were bought separate from the cookhouse. Fairway Market let us charge and the Forest Service would shop for us there. Mom would send them a check once a month.

We still had gas lanterns and kerosene lamps, but that was okay. We had a battery powered radio and Mom would listen to Arthur Godfrey's "Breakfast Hour" and Bing Crosby. The folks listened to the news too. I don't think the reception was always that great. I liked to

"Big Doug" bringing in the tractor.

listen to "The Lone Ranger."

The summer of 1955 was the last summer we were in there. There was talk and planning of another airstrip soon to be built. Dad was transferred to Sula Ranger Station on the Bitterroot National Forest. Life was much easier for Mom. She could go to town, have conveniences and belong to Women's Club. Dad and Mom enjoyed Sula and so did I.

Dad retired in 1958, and the folks moved back to their home in Hamilton, Montana, where they enjoyed retirement life.

Dad, myself, my brother David and Mom on the back porch of our cabin at Moose Creek R.S.

A TENT?

by Barbara Johnson Baldwin

"Guess they'll have to live in a tent," I heard the men talking and thought it was maybe a joke. Bill Johnson and I had spent three months in a tourist cabin along the Clark Fork River in Thompson Falls, a great place. Then the word came, move to Plains.

We combed the town but there were no rentals. In early 1946 there was no housing and few cars. We managed to get a 1937 two door Ford with no heater and no trunk.

The tent turned out to be quite lovely. It was 14 x 16 feet with a wood floor, screen all around, a lookout cook stove, and thanks to a kind relative a refrigerator. Water came from a spigot in the yard, and the outhouse was out back.

It was a good summer, and we had the promise of a rental house when the current renters could move into their newly built home. You know how that goes, later rather than sooner.

Fall came early and chilly; we lowered the flaps and added a small barrel stove and watched the icicles form on the tent walls. We held out in that wall tent until Thanksgiving, when I went to Hamilton to stay with my sister. Our first child was born December 8th.

A friend in Plains said, "You'll look back on this as the best of times. No windows to wash." True, so true.

Bill Johnson
Plains, Montana

Barbara Johnson
shingling the "outhouse."

THE START OF MY LIFE
AS THE WIFE OF A FOREST RANGER
by Barbara Sanderson

We were living in San Marcos, Texas, when Sandy, my husband found that he had enough points to allow him to leave the Eighth Air Force. He had finished his tour of duty in England as a navigator in B-24's.

Missoula was our destination when we left San Marcos. Sandy went to see the Regional Forester to apply for a job. He was sent to the Princeton Ranger station on the St. Joe Forest as an Assistant Ranger under Charlie Powell. Princeton was a small town with a population of 25. I had stayed in Missoula to wait for him to find us a place to live. When I finally got tired of waiting I called him and told him to meet the train in St. Maries as I was coming. I soon found that there were no rentals, but when we got to the station I noticed a 14 x 16 foot tent in the yard and said "why not live there?" In the barn we found a door, a spring and

14 x 16 tent "winterized"
Princeton R.S.

mattress and some tin plates and pots and pans. In 1945 the Forest Service didn't seem to worry about housing families. We lived in the tent from July till the first of November when we moved into the cookhouse. In April, we moved back to the tent with our two month old son, Alan. He was an easy baby to care for as the shadows from the tree leaves always put him to sleep at nap time.

Refrigerators and washing machines were not available at first, so

I washed clothes in a tub with the help of a washboard and had made a cold storage box by digging a hole at the side of the tent and putting an orange crate in. I used a damp tarp to keep it cool. Finally we found a water tank to store water and ran a pipe down the hill to give us running water in the tent. We also built a shelf and clothes closet. Our sanitary facilities were outdoors and were a bit chilly to use in the winter. The shower was in the woodshed and was partitioned off from the wood storage. When one wanted to take a shower it was necessary to haul a hose up a ladder to fill the water tank and to build a fire in the small stove below. I always took my shower during the day while the crew was away from the station because of the wide cracks in the wall.

Summer of 1945,
Barbara and Sandy.

After another winter in the cookhouse we once again moved to the tent. In the meantime we had received a priority to buy both a refrigerator and washing machine. We didn't get much use of them because before long we were transferred to Magee Ranger Station on the Coeur d'Alene Forest. At Magee the light plant only operated from 7 to 10 p.m. We bought an old Maytag washer with a gas engine and a kerosene refrigerator to replace our electric ones which we had sold.

Sandy was now the Ranger and our Forest supervisor was Karl Klehm. He learned that I had ridden horses when I was younger and told me that I could ride the stock when I felt like doing so.

Joan, our second child was born while we were at Magee causing some excitement as it took two hours of driving over the old Tepee Summit road to Coeur d'Alene.

We were fortunate to live at Magee in a three bedroom log house with an indoor bathroom and running water. We had many contacts with bears so I kept close watch over our children. On quiet weekends, they lounged on the hillside or in the yard. One came every night to raid the cookhouse garbage and one robbed the meathouse. Sandy shot him in the middle of the night. He was an old garbage bear. The children loved to see the horses and mules and feed them grass. They liked to go to the river and toss rocks in it. We moved to Magee in the spring and left the week before Thanksgiving and spent winters in Missoula or Coeur d'Alene.

Princeton Ranger Station
St. Joe National Forest
Sanderson Family 1947
Barbara, Alan & Sandy.

Opening Magee R.S. April 1947. Karl Klehm – Forest Supervisor, Coeur d'Alene National Forest.

HOME IN THE OLD CCC RECREATION HALL
by June Finch

After three years of duty with the Army during World War II, Tom came home and I eagerly looked forward to life together on a Ranger District. However, he accepted a job with the Experiment Station in Missoula, which meant our new son and I saw little more of him than when he was on occupation duty in Japan. He and his crew were "on survey" and I do believe they surveyed every square inch of the state of Idaho! Then came the day five years later when he called in great excitement .... he had been offered a job as one of two assistant rangers on the Sullivan Lake District in Washington. Most exciting for him was the location. Sullivan Lake is 100 miles north of Spokane and 13 miles from the Canadian border, and it had been a favorite camping and fishing spot for his family when he was growing up. It is truly a beautiful spot and I've often said every young forester should have some time there. It is also 8 miles from the nearest town, Metaline Falls, reached by a narrow, winding and climbing road inhabited by logging trucks, lumber trucks, and by a neighbor lady who frequently drove like a bat out of hell up the middle of the road. The town itself left a lot to be desired, but it did have a good school where our 6 year old son was to start in the first grade. A school bus picked him up each morning at 8 and seldom brought him home before 5 – a long day for first graders.

The only Forest Service dwelling was occupied by the Ranger and his wife and was situated across the air strip and near the Station itself. Our side of the air strip had been a CCC encampment which was now occupied by Diamond Match workers as well as Forest Service crews. Our quarters were in the former CCC recreation hall which consisted of 2 apartments with a long store room in between. We had acquired a cat which was welcomed by us to keep us free of the mice that often slipped in. At the far end of the storeroom was a high stack of old mattresses and to my chagrin I soon found those mattresses provided a safe refuge for the cat – she was as upset by mice as I was!

The exterior of our building had at one time been stained green. Age had weathered it to a dismal faded olive – always good for either a head-shaking laugh or a sympathetic pat on the shoulder whenever family and friends arrived for a first visit. One day I was delighted to find a small warehouseful of odds and ends of paint, and a great transformation was about to start on the interior of our new home. After painting all the woodwork a high gloss white, I did the bedrooms in pastel blue and the kitchen in sunshiney yellow, only the second of a string of yellow kitchens to follow me right up through today. All of the outside walls were wainscoted in cedar paneling, so on that wall of the kitchen I was able to put up a strawberry print wall paper we found in Spokane. The living room presented more and larger problems, but eventually we had a home we were happy with and the contrast with the outside only made the inside look even better, or so I told myself. Then one day Tom's brother came to visit, made an appraising look around and said, "You know, with a little elbow grease you kids could have a pretty cute place!" (Not my favorite brother-in-law!)

Shep & "Cocoa" (bear cub)
family house in background.

One evening shortly after our arrival I was cooking dinner and happened to glance out the window in time to watch a black bear, nose in the air, sniffing his way up the driveway. I'm not sure what changed his mind, but I whipped out the storeroom door, ran to a neighbor's where our son had gone to play, and the bear was already there, patiently waiting for the children to vacate the sandbox where they apparently were on his straight line between two points. Bear appearance became fairly routine, but about the only problems they caused us were the cans of garbage they sorted through nightly, leaving only the coffee grounds and the banana peelings.

An another occasion, our son and I decided to walk over to the Ranger Station to meet Tom. I thought he might be happy to see us, but I wasn't prepared for the excitement we had created. It seems that Diamond Match fellows were sitting on their bunkhouse porch and saw us taking off across the airstrip. As we reached the middle of the field, the men were horrified to see a cougar stalking us through the grass. Calling to us would only make us run, which would have triggered the cougar to really attack, so I guess all they could do was watch our progress and alert Tom by phone. We arrived safely at the office, none the worse for our cougar encounter, but I was reminded of it recently when we watched a cougar stalking a doe and fawn outside our yard at The Finch Forte.

Through the years, we moved to other Ranger districts, each with its own good memories, but Sullivan Lake will always be most special. I have a feeling there are some middle-aged men out there who look back fondly on school bus trips on Tuesday to their Cub Scout clubhouse Tom built, and to the wild sledding rides over forest roads and ending with hot dogs and cocoa at our house.

Since retirement, we have our own 40 acres of timbered land and Tom is now practicing forestry "his way."

Cub Scout pack in front of club house Tom made. (our Cub Scout now 54 yrs. old).

Sullivan Lake Ranger Station Herman Ficke and "Shep".

MOVING, MOVING AND MOVING
by Laurene Engler

In August 1999, George and I attended the 50th anniversary of the Mann Gulch fire to honor the 13 smokejumpers who gave their lives to save our forests. This commemoration of a tragic event brought back many memories of our life during the thirty-six years George worked for the Forest Service.

One could write a book about the next fifty-two years but I'll only touch on the housing we had while working for the Forest Service and the kinds of roads we traveled at that time.

We came to Lincoln, Montana, in May 1947 where George began his career. George came ahead a few days while Carol, our small daughter, and I visited with friends in northern Idaho, where I had taught school in the early 1940's. George met us in Helena and we drove over Flesher Pass to Lincoln. We sat at the top of the pass to view this beautiful country that was to be our new home.

We stayed in a one room cabin near the ranger station, using pots and pans already in the cabin. They were huge, ordinarily used for a fire kitchen but stored in this cabin. We were waiting for a van to bring our things from Naches, Washington. Nothing arrived for a week, then two weeks, then three weeks. Finally, George called the Naches Ranger Station. Oops – the van line had never picked up this load. Our Forest Service friends took care of things, calling Mayflower Van Lines in Yakima. Voila! A van showed up only a few days later. In those days one helped Uncle Sam save every penny possible. Since our furniture would

LINCOLN VALLEY MONTANA

Old Farm House, Lincoln, Montana. 1947.

only fill a small portion of a large van, our things were to be taken from Naches to Yakima and stored until a van would be filled. Then each persons belongings were delivered along the way. This was all a matter of efficiency and saving money. By the time the beds got to us I was sure there wasn't anything efficient about this move and I never knew if there was any money saved.

We set up beds for a night or two, then took them down to move into an old ranch house for the remainder of the summer. Most of this house had not been lived in for years. We cleaned up the bedroom, dining room and kitchen. George had agreed with the owner that "I wouldn't mind gathering the eggs, washing them and washing the cream separator." While I was doing these chores as a favor because our rent would be so "reasonable," George was off to his new job, getting acquainted with the forest and the people he would be working with.

Another interesting thing about this place was the location of the toilet. It was in front of the house in the middle of the bull pasture. The front steps of the house were long gone so one had to be able to jump those three feet to the ground or go out the back door and around the house. Then you had to decide if the animals were far enough away to open the gate, take care of business and get back outside the pasture before one of those BIG animals with the ring in their nose came close. I never did feel comfortable in that place!

The end of this tale came in late summer. There had been a three day rain and Carol and I had been out to dinner with friends. They'd brought us home and we were ready to turn the lights out when I remembered I had not gathered the eggs. We put on our jeans and picked up the egg basket, found a flashlight and were off to the hen house, a block away. I had a brilliant idea. I'd drive the farm panel truck down, hurry with the eggs and be back before we both drowned – it was pouring. We got to the hen house and gathered the eggs with no problems. Then things changed. The little old panel truck was stuck, really stuck. So, I walked a half mile to the store where some kind man offered help. He pulled the panel truck out of the mud, made sure I made it back to the house, and waved a hand "glad to help." George was off somewhere with our car. Rangers frequently provided their own transportation in those days. The next thing I knew I wouldn't have to gather eggs anymore or wash the cream separator. Hurrah! But where to live?

I went home to visit my family in Idaho while George looked for a house suitable for the winter. He found a summer home that we could rent. "Summer home" means a house or cabin built for warm weather. This house had no insulation and very thin walls but it did have a pitcher pump at the kitchen sink and an oil heater in the main room. We happily moved in and merrily went on with our lives. Only later did we realize

SUMMER CABIN, LINCOLN, MONTANA 1947

what a summer cabin was really like. The beds sat in the middle of the room from November to May.

We really enjoyed the year we spent at Lincoln. People were so "real" and friendly. We were transferred to Townsend, Montana, on May 6, 1948, leaving Lincoln about dark. Another one of those efficient moves where we saved every penny we could for Uncle Sam. The van of furniture came that afternoon for the man who was to replace George. George and Ole helped unload the van, carefully setting everything on the porch, then loaded our things into the van and moved Ole's things into the cabin. We finally made it to Helena late evening and found a place to stay, a bit to eat and crawled into bed. The van would arrive in Townsend the following day.

We moved into a tiny house in Townsend that the Forest Service owned. I fell in love with this house immediately – it had indoor plumbing! We spent four years in Townsend.

In 1951 we were transferred to Red Lodge, Montana. We moved into the Ranger Station on Rock Creek, about three miles out of town. Before getting unpacked I was told, "Hold it. We're going to the Sage Creek station in the Pryor Mountains." After sorting the boxes and repacking for the next three months, off we went.

Sage Creek is east of Bridger, Montana, and reached by traveling dirt roads which turned to mud after a shower. We had outside rest facilities, and a gas lamp for light in the evenings. Our seven-year-old daughter thought it was great reading *"Lucretia Ann on the Oregon Trail"* by lamplight.

We moved back to Red Lodge for the winter. Housing was difficult to find in the years immediately following WW II. We rented a house that had been "modernized" by taking out the coal stoves in every room and replacing them with one gas heater in the living room. That left the rest of the house pretty chilly.

Just after Thanksgiving we found an apartment that we thought would do until we could find something else. Most of our furniture was stored at the Rock Creek station because we could not get it around the square turns in the stairway. Just after Thanksgiving we were on our way again. Sounded good – there would be government housing. About mid-December our furniture at Rock Creek was moved to a garage in town. A big snow storm was in progress and word was "If you don't get your things out of there now, you probably won't get them out 'til June."

January 2, 1952, found us on our way to the Fort Howes Ranger Station, 25 miles south of Ashland, Montana. On the way we passed our van full of furniture which had slid off the road into the barrow pit. I was sure there wouldn't be much to unpack, but miraculously everything was intact when we unpacked.

There was another move proving how efficient the Forest Service was. The van arrived at Fort Howes in the afternoon. The man leaving the station was waiting for the van and help, as they were having their things packed by the van lines. After a long afternoon of staying out of the way and trying to keep warm, the boxes and barrels were packed and the Simpsons were on their way. Our furniture was still on the porch.

George and the Assistant Ranger set up the beds and parked everything else in the living room. Then they were off up the creek. The Assistant Ranger was buying chickens and George thought he should go along and meet the folks who were permittees.

Fort Howes was the ranger district where I began experimenting with recipes using canned meats and fish. For the first year at this station we had a generator so we could have lights in the evening. However, we had a coal stove to cook on and no refrigeration. We had to travel 60 miles over dirt roads and fourteen miles of gravel road and a few more miles of pavement to go to town for anything to eat. "Spam Hawaiian" or "Tuna ala King" were necessities because the trips to town were limited.

Weather played a large part in the plan to go to town. Even a light shower turned that gumbo to mud that we just couldn't travel in.

In March when I returned from my father's funeral, George met me in Billings where we stayed overnight because the roads were "gummy." At 5:30 a.m. the next morning we were up and headed for the Ranger Station before the sun came up and the frozen road began to thaw.

Once while living at this remote station one of the children was very sick. We phoned the doctor in Sheridan, Wyoming, for help. He told us to stay home and "keep that baby warm, George can get Ilene Tate." "I'll phone her and she can give the baby a penicillin shot." Ilene lived nine miles and nine gates from the ranger station. By evening Ilene had been "fetched," the gates opened and closed many times, the shot had been given and our baby seemed much better.

Much of our entertainment as a family was spent doing things outdoors, such as picking wild plums, gooseberries or just watching wildlife going to and from the spring. The spring was five miles from our house, but a can of spring water was a treat as the water at the station had a lot of soda in it. Therefore we drank "green tea" and "awful coffee" most of the time. Other people in the community would bring their own water when they came for a party or church services at the station.

Our school on Otter Creek was very small having only eight students. There were very few library books and we could not use the public library in Sheridan because we were not Wyoming residents. I was telling this to a permittee's wife and she said, "Oh, Laurene, you can request books from the state library in Missoula. They'll mail them to you and you pay the postage back." I was astounded at the number of books and the wonderful selections they made for us. My life had been saved again!

June 1955 I was packing again, this time we were returning to Red Lodge, Montana. Housing was still difficult to find but we found a house to rent and later that summer we bought a house. We were having some work done on the house including insulating, new bathroom fixtures, cabinets and flooring in the kitchen. We moved into our house on February 14, 1956. A blizzard was raging outside; another move in a Montana winter!

After moving into and out of eighteen houses and eleven stations we moved to Great Falls in 1967 into our nineteenth home. George was supervisor there for nine years on the Lewis and Clark National Forest.

This is a brief sketch of my life as a Forest Service wife. Muddy roads, long distances to "anywhere" and almost non-existent housing provided many memorable experiences.

Note: Shelly Engler, daughter of George and Laurene Engler, drew the line sketches to go with her mother's story.

A GOOD LIFE
by Marty Johnson
(Mrs. Art Johnson)

As a Forest Service wife and mother, I raised two sons in a U.S. Forest Service career environment. It was good for us, and good for the boys. As a family we formed life-long friendships. Our son's treasured and gained from the people we met, and from the places we lived. It was not a city oriented perspective, it was back-country, fields and forests. How lucky we were!

We have talked to other Forest Service families who experienced this same good life. A nurse at Sacred Heart Hospital in Spokane shared these same experiences. She, too, was raised in a Ranger District environment and said it was the best. The Forest Service isn't just a 100 year old agency – it's a center for an organization charged with the responsibility to manage a segment of our public forest lands. The goal is simple: "The greatest good, for the greatest number, in the long run."

When Art graduated from the University of Idaho, Forest Service jobs were scarce. In 1949 he had worked as a fire guard on the Kingston Ranger District, Coeur d'Alene National Forest. At that time the Forest Service, in cooperation with the Idaho State Forestry Department, provided fire protection on 200 thousand acres of State and Private land west of Rose Lake, Idaho. The area extended all the way to Harrison on Coeur d'Alene Lake. It was a challenging job and we met a lot of people, and suppressed a few wild fires.

As a result of this four month summer job, Art was offered a ten month appointment on the Kingston Ranger District. It was the beginning of a twenty-seven year Forest Service career. Clarence Stillwell was the Ranger at Kingston and Vern Hamre his assistant. Again, this was the start of life-long friendships.

In June of 1950 we started house hunting in the Kingston area. It was tough. For starters we moved into a one-room tourist cabin. There was no running water and no toilet, water was 200 feet away. Our sons were four years old and four months. Bathing was a problem. We bought a heater you dropped in a galvanized tub and waited for results. It was fun, and we were there a couple of months. Later, the same summer we moved up a level or two. Vern and Jean helped us move. The move was to a converted "chicken coup." It at least had running cold water and again, an outside toilet. Vern and Art moved it to a "new hole" with his jeep. This, too, lasted as a home for a couple of months.

Later we got a break. Don Hazelbaker decided to go to work for Pack River Lumber Company at Bonners Ferry. This opened his Kingston Ranger District job and fortunately there was a CCC barracks apartment on the Ranger Station. It had hot water and a shower stall. The district crews next door shared a common shower wall with us. We could hear them shower and they could hear us.

It wasn't all perfect, but we had a wood stove and coal heater, and almost everything was under one roof. The place was not insulated, however, and on cold winter nights Art would set the alarm and feed coal to our heater. Even this didn't keep house plants from freezing inside our dwelling.

After a year, the Hamre's were transferred and the Skip Stratton's moved in, he as assistant ranger. Art had a new hunting buddy for two years. When the Strattons left, Art became assistant ranger. We were set for life, except Carl Krueger; Forest Supervisor decided Art most move on to receive promotions. Carl Klehm was at Sandpoint and offered Art an assistants job at Sandpoint. Shorty McNeely was ranger. After five months at Sandpoint, Art was assigned as assistant at Bonners to replace Gus Verdall, where Arnie Nousanen was ranger. One month later, Art was assigned as ranger at Calder, Idaho, on the St. Joe National Forest. And five months later to the Avery Ranger District to replace Mitch Philips. Avery was a promotion and we treasure the experience and the community. It was Forest Service, Milwaukee Railroad and Potlatch. About 300 of us in total – great people.

In 1960, Avery schools were not offering what we needed for our oldest son Bill's education. We requested a transfer and took the move to the Clearwater National Forest. Ralph Space was supervisor and we found a home. At Orofino we fortified ourselves and avoided all transfers. Coeur d'Alene was to be our retirement area, but Orofino took its place.

A WONDERFUL LIFE
by Marian B. Emerson

My life as a Forest Service wife began May 27, 1950, with my wedding to John Emerson at the end of my senior year at University of Montana. We honeymooned in Yellowstone Park and then flew into Big Prairie Ranger Station on the Flathead National Forest for the summer. John would again work as a dispatcher (and "other duties as assigned") as he had done the previous two years and I had been hired to take the daily weather and report it to the Kalispell Supervisor's office and to cook for VIP personnel whenever they came into Big Prairie.

Taking the weather was no problem, but I was a little daunted about the cooking as I did not know how to cook, especially on a wood range!

John and I flew into Big Prairie via a private small plane flown by Teddy Van. My father asked Teddy if he could fly in and out to see where we were going to live. When we left Kalispell we had to circle and circle to get high enough to cross the Swan Range. It was my first trip in a small plane and I wasn't too secure. It wasn't til later I found the reason for circling was that the passengers and luggage were too heavy.

It was a beautiful sunny day and the scenery was awesome for me. When we landed the crew was out to greet us. After introductions, John said, "Marian will cook dinner for you." As my mouth dropped, John said in an aside "I'll help you," and after taking our belongings to the cabin that was to be our residence for the summer he disappeared not to reappear til the dinner bell sounded!! I also found that the meat comes in quarters and hung in a nearby meat house. He took the quarter down and sliced off steaks for everyone. There was probably 8 to 10 crew members so I completed the dinner with boiled potatoes and canned green beans. All the food was brought in from Kalispell by the aerial observer once a week if the weather allowed.

Later that summer I even learned to bake pies. Once I baked lemon pies for a group of Regional Office fellows and one of them came to the kitchen and asked for the recipe for his wife! Sure made me feel good, although I knew he was just being nice.

That summer was a wonderful experience for me since I was a town girl and I stayed in there for 3 months without ever going out. Even John went out on a training session. I did learn to cook on a wood stove which stood me in good stead when we moved to Grangeville, Idaho, and housing was extremely hard to find. We had to live in the Vet's Housing apartments – one that only had a wood stove until we could find a house.

We would fly fish the South Fork of the Flathead in the evenings and the weekends. Pretty easy to catch trout in those days and we could count on fish every time we went. We hiked and rode horses on the weekends. I picked wild strawberries, did a little housework and lots of reading. In the evenings we would play cards with any of the crew that

Plane at Big Prairie R. S. brought in supplies and people.

happened to be in the station. A wonderful life!

Whenever the packer left with the mule string, everyone still at the station would sit along the airfield fence and watch. It was quite a procedure to mantee the supplies and equipment (like a stove and shovels). One day as Jerry started up the trail with the supplies for the trail crew at Salmon Lake, something set the mules off and they bucked everything off. It took Jerry the rest of the day to collect and re-mantee the supplies. He left the next morning with very docile animals and no trouble.

One night we had a spectacular lightning storm. Lightning was coming down all around us so John went out the back door and watched for strikes and I watched out the front door. About midnight the ranger, Glenn Mariott, sent Jim Wahl back to his lookout, Jumbo, so that he would be there at sunrise to look for smokes. Made excitement for the crew.

The old log cabin that we had that summer had been fixed up for us with a new inside bathroom. This cabin had a kitchen with a wood stove, table and chairs, another room with a bed and a rocking chair and the bathroom. John and I put up the sheet rock in the kitchen. We used a gas lantern at night and we would sit in the kitchen and the mice would come out and play on the counter in the gas light. We would even throw books at them but they would come right back. I washed clothes in the

Marian wading in South Fork Flathead River late June, Big Prairie 1950.

View of dwellings at Big Prairie. First building on left is where we lived summer of 1950, next is bunkhouse and office on far right.

bunkhouse with a gas washer. The food perishables were in the office/warehouse and we would take what we need for each meal. John would have to slice the meat we needed. Mostly beef, ham, bacon and chicken the day the plane came in. I did learn to cook with the use of *Better Homes and Garden* cook book that I use to this day. I also learned to bake pies but couldn't seem to make a cake until cake mixes became popular in the 60's.

The same plane that brought the supplies would also bring in the mail. One time I wrote my mother in Kalispell that I needed a recipe for pancakes, and two weeks later I received the recipe. Only her last instruction was to "add milk til John tells you to stop." I couldn't understand how John would know, but later found it was an "old wives tale" from her grandmother.

Just before we left Big Prairie the early hunting season was starting. The evening before opening day, Glenn took John and I out to show how he could bugle elk. It was exciting to hear the elk returning Glenn's bugling and coming closer and closer. I could hear the elk crashing through the woods and brush and the smell getting stronger and stronger. The next morning Glenn and John took off early with their guns and Glenn bugled and bugled and bugled – and not a sign or sound of that elk or any other elk. Always have wondered how that elk knew when hunting season started?

One time in August Fred Neitzling, Flathead Supervisor, came in to Big Prairie and I was cooking supper for him. I was outside cooking and he came over and introduced himself. We were talking and he said, "I understand that you don't like it in here." I burst into tears and he hurriedly left to find John to tell him that he was teasing me and I started crying and that John had better get home or the steaks would be burnt! I learned later that he was a big tease, but don't think he ever tried to tease me again.

When we left in the fall to return to school, for John to finish his senior year, the mail plane took our baggage to Kalispell. John and I rode horses out to Holland Lake staying overnight at Shaw Cabin. My folks met us and that ended a wonderful summer. Now fifty years later, I have such good memories of that summer. I loved the isolation and the beauty of the wilderness.

Honeymoon couple
33 years later. (1983).

EARLY YEARS OF A FOREST SERVICE CAREER
A PARTNER'S PERSPECTIVE
by Eva Jean Worf

Following is a brief synopsis of the first seven years of Bill's Forest Service career from my perspective. I could write volumes more but these glimpses will give the reader the flavor of those exciting challenging years.

Bill graduated from the University of Montana with a degree in Forestry/Range in the spring of 1950. He was offered a career conditional appointment on a range survey crew in the Bridger National Forest, headquartered at Kemmerer, Wyoming. He had hoped to work in Region One but jobs were very hard to come by so we agreed he should accept it.

We knew that this would be a short time assignment so we stored most of our belongings at my folks place in Billings. Then piled our children (Gary 2 ½ and Gloria nearly 1) into a 1939 Nash (2 door sedan), along with the clothing and equipment we needed for the summer, and headed for Wyoming. It was an unusually hot June day as we crossed the high desert over South Pass and the Nash suffered from vapor lock about every 25 miles. Bill found that he could blow into the tank and get the gasoline past the vapor. By the time we limped into Kemmerer, Bill had a dark ring around his mouth that took a lot of soap and hard scrubbing to remove. We had not been able to line up housing ahead of time so, we camped, the first night, in the F.S. warehouse.

The following morning we started to search for more permanent housing. All we could find was a small (three room) apartment that opened up on a busy and dusty alley. Luckily, the landlord allowed us to have our children play in his fenced yard. As I recall, we paid $50.00 per month plus utilities – a stiff price in those days – salary for a GS5 at the first step was $3,100.00. The kitchen was fitted with a small refrigerator and a wood burning range. Luckily I had been raised on an eastern Montana ranch with one of these ranges, so had some experience to go on. The heat, when winter came on, was a pot-bellied coal stove. There was no insulation or storm windows. When the winter winds began to blow – the curtains would stand out from the windows – but I'm getting ahead of my story.

Bill and I spent Saturday and Sunday getting settled in, buying groceries and exploring the town. Early Monday morning the crew, under leadership of Hap Johnson, took off for the Survey Camp at the Snyder Basin Station on the Big Piney Ranger District. The kids and I were left alone for 5 days each week. I had never learned to drive a car (and did not want to start) but that was not much of a problem, because the grocery store and post office were only about 2 blocks away. I soon met a great new friend, Grace LeGrand. She had a son about the same age as Gary and her husband hauled railroad ties, so was gone a great deal. We had a lot in common and hit it off well.

My folks drove down from Montana for a visit and brought more of our things so that it helped make our living a bit easier. We all went up to a campground near the Survey Camp, so that we could spend a weekend with Bill.

Bill came home one Friday night very excited. The Forest Service Chief, Lyle Watts, Regional Forester, Forest Supervisor and other dignitaries had spent a couple of nights with the crew at their camp. This was a very thrilling experience for the new forester and he could talk about little else that weekend.

The field survey ended in October when snow flakes began to fall so I finally had Bill home every night. He worked in the office compiling and summarizing the data that had been collected all summer. Winter hit Kemmerer with a vengeance and that is when we discovered the lack of insulation and storm windows that I referred to earlier. The pot-bellied stove consumed a lot of coal, but we were comfortable.

We got a real scare in November. We were out one Saturday night celebrating the Marine Corps birthday. Bill was a Marine in World War II and had signed up in the Marine Corps, inactive reserve, when he was discharged. While he was in college, he joined ROTC to earn a little more money. He had received a commission in the Army as 2nd Lieutenant and assumed that, as a result, he was out of the Marine Reserves. During the party he mentioned to the local recruiting Sergeant that he was still getting correspondence from the Marine Corps. The Sergeant said "I believe you are still in the Reserves! You better come in on Monday and I'll see what I can find out." Bill did that and they found that he was actually still in the Reserves. The Sergeant started the ball rolling to get Bill discharged. Bill came home for lunch and, while we were eating, we received a special delivery letter with orders telling him to report for active duty at Camp Pendleton, California. We really hit the panic button! It meant a fast track to the front lines in Korea. After some long telephone negotiations, the Marine Corps finally agreed to discharge Bill on the condition that he immediately get in the "active" Army Reserve. That meant he had to drive to Salt Lake City for drill every two weeks (about 260 miles round trip). Of course, that sure beat having him go off to war.

We drove to Montana for Christmas with our folks but the winter was otherwise pretty uneventful.

On to Heber City, Utah.

In late winter Bill was transferred to the Heber District on the Uinta National Forest. My brother Ray brought our stored things down from Montana, picked up our stuff in Kemmerer and hauled it down to Heber for us. We found a very small (two tiny bedrooms, living room and kitchen) but snug house only about one-half block from the office.

The District had previously been two – Lake Creek and Current Creek Districts. The Lake Creek District had been classified as GS9 and the Current Creek as GS7. The combined District became the first GS11 District in Region 4 and Andy McConkie was the Ranger. Bill was a GS5 assistant. It is interesting to compare the staffing then, and now. Andy and Bill were the only permanent full time employees on the District. There was no District Clerk so Bill did the filing, manual maintenance, janitorial work, etc. in addition to his field work – mostly nights and week-ends. Andy did the typing and bookkeeping. There was one permanent/part time employee, Tennis Poulson, who worked about 9 months per year and was responsible for timber sales, improvement maintenance, etc.

The District combination had been done to enable the F.S. to tackle the severe range problems that existed. The new District had an obligation for about 30,000 sheep and 7,000 cattle. Most of these ran in common – sheep and cattle used the same range. The range had great potential, but it was deteriorating badly. They wanted Bill to determine the sustainable capacity and provide the information to support needed adjustments. It was a huge job for one person, so Bill was out in the field all week and the kids and I were alone again. Once in the spring of 1951, Bill was due in on Friday night but did not show up. He had gone into Current Creek – about 3 hours of hard drive from Heber. There was no radio and no phone. It turned out that Bill had started home about 6 p.m. when he met a herd of sheep that was headed on to the Forest. Bill knew that he should get a count on them, but they had already bedded down for the night. So, Bill bedded down also and counted them when they started to move at daylight. He found that there were about 100 head more than allowed by the permit. In the meantime I had called Andy McConkie and he headed out to look for Bill as soon as it got light. He met Bill just after he had completed the count. Over the years, I learned to accept the fact that unavoidable delays could happen when Bill was working in the Forest, but I still worried!

Bill had to follow through with his commitment to remain active in the Army Reserve. They finally had him establish a unit in Heber City. That took a lot of time but at least he did not have to commute to Salt Lake City.

Forest Service business and family life clashed again in June of 1952. Our 3rd child (Ron) was due at precisely the same time that all new Foresters were scheduled for a two week orientation trip to the Regional Office and Idaho National Forests. The kids and I traveled up to Montana and Ron was born in Miles City June 7, 1952.

Bill's range studies kept him in the field most of the time. The District was pretty well covered with low standard roads so he was able to stay in and work out of one of the three field stations. There were a lot of horse days, but no packing. The children and I joined him at one of the cabins quite often, during the three years we were on the District. Our favorite one was the Hub station in Strawberry Valley. The kids all fell in love with the horse Bill used most of the time – Old Smoky – and he loved them. They could all pile on him and he treated them very gently. We have a picture in our family album with four children on him – Gary, Gloria and two of their friends.

Late in the summer of 1952, the new F.S. Chief Dick McArdle, visited the Uinta N.F. and Supervisor Jim Jacobs planned a family picnic at the Lodgepole Campground near the head of Daniel's Canyon on the Heber District. Chief McArdle was famous for his ability to remember names and he liked to show that talent off. While visiting before the dinner was served, he made it a point to meet and talk briefly with everyone. Then, as we came through the chow line, he stood there and called everyone by name. Bill and I were near the end of the line and as we came through he said "and here are Bill and Eva Jean Worf and their children Gary and Gloria – but wait a minute there is one member of this family missing – Where is Ronald?" I told him that Ronnie was asleep in the car. We were all very impressed. I did not see him again until several years later at a national meeting of the Society for Range Management in Salt Lake City. Even though I was not with Bill at the moment – he knew me instantly.

Bill's work was being watched very closely by the entire community. There were about 300 permittees – some with only 2 or 3 head of cattle. Nearly everyone in Heber was either in a permittee family or related to someone who was. Every one was apprehensive about what might be coming. The dynamics was further complicated by the fact that both the presidents of the National Cattlemen's Association, Levi

Montgomery, and the National Wool Growers Association, Don Clyde live in Heber. By the end of the second field season, it was clear that major adjustments in use would be needed. This meant that about 65% of the animal unit months had to be removed. Apprehension turned to hostility that even I felt. We had developed some very good friends who stood by me. We still correspond with most of these. However, during our last year in Heber, it became more comfortable to do most of our shopping in Provo – some 30 miles away. The Regional Forester and Chief were under heavy political pressure and a parade of range scientists came by to look at Bill's work. It apparently passed muster because support at the top never wavered. Adjustments went forward and after we moved on.

Bill's thirst for adventure added a new source of worry for me. He used the balance of his GI Bill entitlement to get his pilot license. He then joined a local flying club and spent a lot of hours poking around the mountains in one of the Club's two planes. It owned a 65 horsepower Aeronca and a little Air-coupe.

Our fourth child, Brent, was born August 12, 1953. We were outgrowing the little 2 bedroom house so rented a larger one in the fall of 1953. It had 3 bedrooms and a coal fired stoker furnace. Bill had to go to Coronado Naval Base for amphibious warfare training. My mother came and stayed with the kids so I could go along. We rented a small apartment in the Coronado Beach Motel and made a second honeymoon out of it. I saw the ocean for the first time. Bill took me for a walk on the beach the first night we were there but I was terrified! I could hear the surf and was afraid I would fall in and drown. We were moving up in our housing and of course it was almost time to transfer again.

On to Whiterocks

In the spring of 1954, Bill was promoted to District Ranger on the Whiterocks District of the Ashley National Forest. This was a GS9 District. Bill replaced George Walkup who had been Ranger on that same District for 32 years.

We moved to the beautiful Elkhorn Ranger Station, located just inside the Forest boundary on Farm Creek about 8 miles north of the Whiterocks trading post. It is about 25 miles to Roosevelt and 40 miles to Vernal where the Supervisors headquarters is located. Bill Hurst was Supervisor and he had a permanent full time staff of 4 people: Chief Clerk, Administrative Officer and C&M Foreman. There were also two junior Foresters headquartered in Vernal that worked for the four District

Rangers. Each ranger received about ½-man year. None of the Districts had a clerk. I remember that the total budget for Bill's district (beyond his salary) was about $8,000.00 per year. This had to cover everything such as equipment rental, travel, administrative improvement maintenance, trail maintenance, range improvement maintenance. Needless to say, there was not a lot of room for extravagance.

Grazing permittees and timber purchasers were not sure what to make of this "kid" that had been sent to replace the tough, 65-year-old George Walkup. Bill Hurst was taking Bill around Vernal to introduce him to key folks. He spotted Floyd Perry walking down the street and pulled over to talk to him. Floyd was President of the Mosby Mountain Cattle Association and a grizzled, bow-legged cowboy about 60 years old. When Hurst introduced Bill, Floyd looked him up and down and told the Supervisor, "Hell, he won't last as long as Walkup did." A few days later Bill met the Farm Creek Association herd of cattle trailing up the road to the Forest. He counted the cattle as they trailed by his truck then walked up to introduce himself to the Association President, Ben Brown. Ben remained mounted. They shook hands and Ben said, "We was expecting someone with a bit more experience!" The word about Bill's range studies on the Heber District had preceded him. He set up a date, soon after the cattle went on, to ride the Farm Creek Allotment with the permittees. They met at the Association cabin. Bill hauled his horse up in his truck. He unloaded his horse and tightened his saddle, but before he could get mounted the entire Association, about 8 and all mounted, gathered around him. Bill shook hands with each of them, and told them that he was looking forward to working with them. Ben Brown said "We are also looking forward to a good positive relationship. We'll get along fine as long as you don't start talking about reducing our permits." Bill laughed and told them that there would be no talk about cutting permits as long as the range was in satisfactory condition and improving. I don't believe Bill saw any serious problems on the cattle ranges on the District. Relationships with the cattle permittees seemed to be quite good. The high sheep range was another matter. I think there were about 15 bands of sheep grazing on the District along the top of the Uinta mountains. Most of this grazing was taking place above 10,500 feet in elevation. I remember Bill shaking his head when he came back from his first pack trip into the high country. He had a deep concern about the effect grazing was having on the fragile alpine type. He worked hard to try to find the best way to deal with the situation. He asked Mont Lewis, the Region's top expert in the alpine type, to come out and advise him. Mont was there several times. Bill also called in watershed research scientists, Bus Croft and Lincoln Ellison. Bill's conclusion was that this alpine country (above timberline) simply should not be grazed by anything but wildlife.

Now back to our family situation. The house had two bedrooms on the ground floor and two that had been finished in the attic. These were accessed by a "pull down" stairway, from the center hallway. There was a nice fireplace in the living room, but the principle heat source was an oil fired space heater in the living room. We replaced a wood range in the kitchen with a "Magic Chef" bottled gas range and a trash burner. Our water source was a spring located high on the mountain. The CCC boys had dug in line over one mile long. The water was cold and wonderful! The first summer we were there, the water quit flowing while Bill was off fighting a small fire. He came home dirty and tired but had to fix the problem before he could take a shower. He checked the spring and everything was fine so he started walking down the line, which ran through one pasture on the Farm Creek Cattle Allotment. Because of the fall in the line (the head) it had been necessary to provide two pressure release points. This had been done by constructing concrete boxes about 4 foot square and 5 feet deep. The water simply flowed into the box through an open end pipe, then it was picked up by another pipe and went on down the line. These boxes had been covered with a water tight lid constructed by heavy wooden plank. The upper one had been covered by soil and the wood had rotted over the 20 years since its construction. Bill found the problem right there! A cow had fallen through the lid – luckily with both front feet. Dirt and rotted wood had plugged the outlet. The cow could not extract herself and the tank was overflowing. I did not see it, but Bill said it was a real mess. He pulled the cow out with his pick-up, cleaned out the tank and we were back in business.

The administrative site included (besides the house) an office, warehouse/garage, above ground cellar, and a 4 horse barn complete with hay mow. There was about 40 acres of irrigated pasture. The Government stock included two horses (Socks and Hatchet Head) and 2 mules. In addition we had a Jersey cow "Bossy" for milk, her calves, which eventually became beef, a couple of pigs and a small horse for Gloria. This was a small blood bay mare which Gloria called "old Red." We also inherited a flock of domestic geese from George Walkup. They provided several scrumptious goose dinners. The care of this menagerie belonged to the kids and me when Bill was away. One thing I refused to do was milk the cow. She produced more milk than we could use so, when Bill was home, he would take what we needed, then let the calf have the balance. When he was going to be gone on a trip, he would take most of it and stock pile it in the cooler. Then when he was gone the calf would get it all. Actually the care of the animals was not a big chore. Bill did the irrigation when he was home and it would usually be OK till he returned.

The station was a great place for children. There was a lot to do. Of course, there were some hazards also. Ron and Brent were particularly attracted to the barn. It was a playhouse, castle, fort, etc. The hayloft was accessed by a ladder fastened to the wall. Brent skinned his nose repeatedly on that ladder. It seemed that he had a scab on his nose almost continually. In spite of the hazards there was only one serious accident. Ron fell from a tree, in the yard, and hit his head on the sidewalk. Bill was home at the time and we rushed Ron to the Doctor in Roosevelt. X-rays showed no fracture but he had a large bump on his forehead and both eyes were blackened. This later developed into a hemorrhagic cyst and brain surgery more than 18 months later. I'll cover that when I write about our tour in the Regional Office in Ogden.

I still had not started to drive a car during our tenure at Whiterocks. That seems odd to me now, but in retrospect it did not present a problem. We had good close neighbors if an emergency had occurred – none did. Also, I had learned to shop for a long period while growing up on our Montana ranch. I learned how to "make do" if we ran out of something. It certainly would not have been any fun taking off for Vernal or Roosevelt by myself in a car, with my young brood.

There is an interesting story around the two mules. They had been obtained as surplus from the Army. They were white and very large – about 17 hands tall. Their names were Buster and Grumpy. They were very gentle. The children loved them and the feeling seemed to be mutual. Whenever Ron and/or Brent would be in the pasture Buster and Grumpy would put their great heads down so the boys could stroke their ears. Those heads were about three feet long. One day in 1956 (Ron was 4 and Brent was 3) Bill looked out his office window and witnessed an amazing sight. They were taking turns riding on Buster's face. Buster would put his head down, the boys would hang onto his ears and wrap their legs around Buster's nose and Buster would raise his head high then deposit the boy gently back on the ground. We had to put a stop to that game, however, for safety reasons.

Gary started school our first year at Whiterocks and Gloria started kindergarten. They rode the bus. Most of the children attending the Whiterocks school were Native Americans. Our children were definitely in the minority. This did not bother Gary in the least, but Gloria was quite apprehensive about having to go to school with children who were "different." We told her that even though they had a different color skin, they really were not "different," she was still not sure. Gloria has dark hair and a dark complexion, especially after a summer in the sun. We had often jokingly called her our little "Indian maid." To reassure her that everything would be OK at school, we told her that she was really part Cheyenne. She accepted this and all apprehension disappeared. Nothing more was ever said on the subject until 1965. We were living in Fairfax, Virginia, and she had a group of friends over for a "slumber party." She came to the living room and asked Bill "Dad, just where does my Indian heritage come from?" She had never forgotten our little white lie in Whiterocks and was very proud of her Indian heritage. Of course, the truth had to be told. She was devastated for awhile. This certainly underscores the tremendous impact parents words can have on young children.

There were two phone services at both the office and in the residence. We had regular commercial service by REA but there was also a single wire (ground return) Forest Service system that connected us to the Altonah District and the Supervisor's office. There was also a branch that went up to the Uinta River Guard Station and another to the Paradise Guard Station. Bill worked out of the Paradise Station quite a bit so that made it possible to keep in touch. When we transferred to Whiterocks, I was pregnant with our fifth child. Mark was born November 1, 1954.

Because most of his District was roadless Bill spent about half the time, during the field season, out in the high country with horse and mules. During those times, I had to assume some "assistant ranger" duties. I logged in phone messages, kept the weather records, and on occasion scaled some timber. There were about 15 small timber purchasers. Most of them cut "mine props" for the mines at Price, Utah. Usually these props were counted and stamped with a US in the woods. When they were hauled to Price they came down the road past the Station. Several times, when an operator got a rush order and Bill had not been able to get the counting done, an operator would stop with a load of unmarked props. I would count while he stamped the US. Once I remember doing this in the dark. I held a flashlight and counted while he swung the hatchet.

A couple of times I had to dispatch a crew to a small fire. Bill had local ranchers signed up as "perdiem guards." They were trained and had tools. When a fire was reported I would call and authorize them to go take care of it.

When I think back on those times on the Ashley, I'm greatly impressed and gratified by the respect I was given, simply because I was the Forest Ranger's wife. I was often called on for advice on everything from raising children to dealing with domestic problems. This was not because I had any special skills but simply because I was "the Ranger's wife." The community was proud of its Forest Service and when friends or relatives were visiting, one of the places to go was to the Elkhorn Ranger Station. That trust and respect held throughout the Basin. It was a legacy established by George Walkup, his wife and the others who had preceded us.

At one point, while we were on the Whiterocks District, Bill came very close to voluntarily ending his F.S. career. We had gotten a new Supervisor, Gil Doll. In those years each Ranger filled out a monthly "Trip and Job" plan that was approved by the Forest Supervisor. Gil decided that he would like to have them done six months at a time. His rationale was that this would allow a better weighing of priorities and minimize frustrations at not being able to get everything done. This seemed like a great idea and Bill spent a lot of time putting the package together. Of course, there was not enough time to do everything so Bill filled up the available paid time each month with jobs and then attached a list of additional jobs that should be done but for which there was not enough time in a 40 hour week. These were sent to the SO and they came back all approved without comment, including the jobs for which there was not enough time. Bill's frustration level ran very high. He had been putting in 20 hours a week or more of non-compensated overtime and had hoped to get a bit of relief. We talked it over and agreed that Bill should air his frustrations with Gil – face to face. Bill actually was very close to resigning! He drove to Vernal and spent several hours with Gil, who explained that he had simply meant that he agreed with Bill's priorities. There was no way of getting more help so "do the best you can!" Bill decided to stick it out. He continued to burn the late hours!

Even though we were perfectly happy at our rural Elkhorn station, powers above decided, the District headquarters should be moved to Roosevelt. A lot was purchased and contracts were let in 1956 to have the dwelling moved to the new lot in town. It was to be remodeled into a "real" 4 bedroom house with a "real" stairway and a furnace. The moving contract called for the house to be moved about June 1. This would allow the remodeling to be completed through the summer so that we could move in before school started. Also, I was expecting our 6th child in November. Short term housing was difficult to find in Roosevelt and we all hated to miss the summer on Farm Creek. There was no remodeling planned for the back bedroom and the mover said it would be

OK for us to move all of our furniture into it. The furniture would to go to Roosevelt in the house. That seemed like a great way to move. We decided to camp right there on the beautiful lawn for the summer. The Forest Service came up with a small trailer house and we pitched two 10' x 12' wall tents for bedroom space for the kids. It looked like a great summer – and it was, except! The house moving contractor ran into trouble somewhere else. The moving day kept being shoved back. We camped there in the yard beside our house all summer long. Of course, we had to get the kids in to start school, so we finally rented a very small two bedroom furnished apartment on the North edge of Roosevelt – the only thing we could find. It was too small for our family so we moved the F.S. trailer house in next to it for additional space. A few days later, we watched our house go by. All the kids went through the measles while we were in this situation. The remodel was completed so that we could move in by Thanksgiving and my folks came down from Montana to help. I missed the move-in fun, however, because I was in the hospital with the birth of our son Keith on November 26. We enjoyed the new house a great deal but that enjoyment was to be short lived. In early spring the Forest Service called again. Bill was promoted to the position of Regional Range Improvement Specialist. We were off to Ogden on another chapter in Bill's F.S. career.

ALONE IN THE WOODS
WITH A MALE INTRUDER
by Layne Spencer

Our first home in the woods was one hour north of Wallace, Idaho. It was nothing at all like the one we were buying on North 5th Street in Coeur d'Alene. We had remodeled the 5th Street. The Forest Service had maintenance of the house at Shoshone Work Station, Bob's second assignment.

The date was April 1951. The two bedroom house set south of the station by about one-half mile and when the river overflowed its banks in the spring it often soaked the house and the two big CCC buildings across the driveway. At that time there was little brush between the house and the river 300 feet away and a nice walk. A beautiful view from our yard.

In the lower flats south of the house was a construction camp filled with single men – each a long ways from home and not much to do with their time off. I was warned about staying close to the house – the only woman for miles.

Their job was to fix the main roads in the area like the one we called Blue Creek Slide – dug out in this slide high above the Coeur d'Alene River. One always stopped to see if the slide had slid before proceeding or a logging truck was coming over that single narrow tract trail and one had to back up! You can tell where I said my daily prayers.

The house was home – two bedrooms, an indoor bathroom and running water – we had it all. A big porch across the back of the house. The back door which was warped from the floods and you couldn't really close it or lock it. After chopping wood you had only to lean on it to get it open – convenient with your arms full of wood for the two stoves that supplied heat for warmth and also to cook our food. Three axes were used daily and not by the man of the house.

We had gas lanterns, no phone, no refrigeration but lots of privacy except for that camp below the house. We used F.S. furniture the first year, which included a iron bed for one to sleep in and cots and old chairs to set on. A long wooden desk/table from someone's office was where we dined in the kitchen. It was bare but convenient.

With various floods, the floor before the bedroom north wall had come off, dropping eight inches in the center. This allowed droves of mice to enter the house as it got quiet and Bob used to prop himself up with pillows and with a sling-shot he managed to wing a few who scampered to get out of his range. We used the battery powered radio for the news and a little music at bedtime.

We shopped in Wallace for supplies once a week. One hour in and one hour to shop and one hour back to camp. Perishables were held in a clamped on lidded can in the creek or under the eaves of the house with a garden hose running water over it constantly. That was our first refrigeration. We saw few bear but mostly by the garbage pit beyond the station. They rarely came near the house.

I was allowed to go walk over to the camp once a day to have a cup of coffee with George "Sally" Falk – the cook, noted for making wonderful food but especially his chocolate pies he is sure he made for 13 cents each. The fifteen minutes allotted coffee time ended much too fast but Sally did allow me to make eleven sport shirts for him that summer on my treadle sewing machine.

Bob was often gone overnight. He warned me against going south toward the construction camp – "stay close to the house!!!" He had been sent to a three day meeting at McGee Ranger Station, an hour north of camp. I was home alone and with no phone or other close contact, it was very scary! The first night was okay. We had a huge battery powered flashlight and it lay on the bed with me – my guard.

The second night I was awakened by someone walking on the back porch – ever so carefully. Immediately I though – what man is out there and why? And Lord don't let him see that the back door doesn't close, or lock!

I can still hear those footsteps slowly and carefully back and forth the full length of the porch, over and over. My heart was in my mouth – and as I got up to look out – the flashlight crashed to the floor and would not work. More careful foot prints back and forth. This person was sure making my hair stand on end. No way to call for help – no phone and hadn't remembered where Bob kept his gun. He hadn't taught me how to use it anyway.

About thirty minutes of this and I was ready for heart failure. At midnight, lights flashed across the living room windows so someone was coming. A pickup stopped in front of the house. Rescue? It was my husband – the meeting was over early so he headed back to camp and home.

My, but he looked good! He listened to my story and quickly went out to see if he could tell which way the man's footprints left the porch. What he found was many large prints left by a bear, beyond and near the back porch – my male intruder!

Paul and Betty Decelle followed us at this site three years later and they found the house remodeled with lots of conveniences and yes, their back door closed.

Our house – 1951.
Shoshone Work
Center. Wallace
Ranger Station.

Vigilante Research Station. We lived here June – Nov. 1951; May 1952 – Nov. 1952; and May 1953 – Nov. 1953. Winter months were spent in Missoula.

A BRIDE AT VIGILANTE
RANGE EXPERIMENT STATION
by June Schmautz

As a bride in June 1951, I went to live at the Vigilante Range Experiment Station in southwestern Montana. Being a former high school teacher and city gal, this place made a tremendous change in my lifestyle. For example, if I wanted to go to the store it meant driving 30 miles on a narrow dirt road to the highway at Alder (just a dot on the map) and then 20 more miles to the small town of Sheridan, Montana.

Not having electricity made the most significant factor in how we lived. This meant no refrigerator, stove, washing machine, lights, etc.

Jack and I drove to town every Saturday to pick up the mail and buy groceries. The fresh meat and vegetables had to be cooked the next day to keep them from spoiling. Eggs were a necessity, but often we waited in town for hours hoping some rancher would bring in eggs for us to buy. Over Jack's objection I talked him into buying six chickens at $1.50 each. I assured my husband that if anyone came to inspect and complained, I'd take the blame. It wasn't long and we were getting six eggs every day. Wow! Then the magpies discovered the feast. I started keeping a loaded shotgun by my door and gave them a good scare now and then. When we moved we butchered the chickens and put them in our locker. A good deal.

Vern and Kay Sylvester often came out Sundays with an ice cream freezer. We followed the snow up the mountains. Ice cream! What a treat! By summer's end we were at a pretty high elevation.

To make it easier for me to start a fire in the kitchen stove, Jack made a mixture of kerosene and sawdust. Directions were to use a scant spoonful. It wasn't long and my can was empty. I went to the shed and made my own mixture. Several days later I commented on how I got such a nice "POP" and the stove lids popped up when I started a fire. I had used high-test gas. My starter can was never empty again! That log shed has been moved to Nevada City, Montana, as part of the recreation of an old western town.

June and Tommy, 1952.

Even washing clothes could be an adventure. Not only did I have to heat the water on the stove and use a scrubboard, but one day as I was hanging clothes on the clothesline, I heard a noise. Looking up I saw two big moose, about ten feet away, watching me. I hightailed it into the house!

We were so far away from everything, and yet we never had more visitors as we did at Vigilante. We bought a case of coffee the first of July and it was gone by the end of September (and I'm not even a coffee drinker). Bill Schowe, (the ranger), often stopped in. When leaving one evening he thanked me for the goodies and coffee and said, "I hate to drink the Ruby River dry to get a good cup of coffee." I asked Jack what he meant. My coffee was too weak, so I learned to serve strong coffee to the guys.

We had a crank up telephone, and every morning I called in weather and fire danger information to the forest headquarters. Our lights were lamps and candles. I ironed clothes by heating the irons on top of the stove. A primitive life indeed.

Those were the good old days. The trouble is, we didn't realize it then. As I look back, they were "good" days.

Jack, Tommy and June with "fur friend," 1954.

MY LOCHSA STORY
by Joyce Rehfeld

I grew up on a farm in Union County, Indiana. In the fifth grade we studied geography by building a big salt map of the United States. I wondered what it would be like to see Idaho where there were no roads, as I knew them. Well! in 1950, while attending Marian College in Indianapolis, I met a tall handsome soldier who was sent from Missoula, Montana, to Camp Atterbury, Indiana, during the Korean War. His name was Bob Rehfeld and he worked at Powell Ranger Station on the Lochsa River in remote Idaho. After we were married in 1953 I spent part or all

Old wood trailer we lived in at Powell Ranger Station, 1953.

of three summers at that station.

My first trip into Powell was a wonder to me – living an old dream. The road, now Highway 12, was gravel all the way from Lolo to the Montana/Idaho State line. It then became a one lane dirt road with grass growing up the middle in many places. We saw a bear cub and a moose. In winter the road was closed by snow so everyone moved into Missoula. The road ended a short way below the Ranger Station.

I felt I was in paradise. It was so beautiful in the canyon on the river. Who needed more than an old work trailer, with hanging bunks, a slivered door, a lookout stove and cold running water – even mice on occasion? The ice box sat out under the bushes, but we had no ice until July. We also had cold storage in the river. Outside, down a short trail, was a flush toilet. Housing was three houses on foundations, two old wood trailers and a wood framed tent. We did laundry in a building behind the Ranger's house. We used a gasoline powered washing machine and water was heated in a wood fired water heater which Bob had to light for me early on my assigned laundry day. Our drier was a washline outside or inside the trailer depending on the weather. The station had no powerlines so used a generator for electricity. During office hours we were asked to turn off lights and refrain from using any electrical appliances so the station radio would work properly. During fire season we usually used lanterns in the evening to conserve power.

We had moose in the pond, bears raiding the garbage cans and attacking the meat Wannigan, mule strings leaving every day, steelhead in Powell Creek, trout from the river for Friday night supper, and huckleberries and blackcaps to be picked. Can you imagine I didn't like the first huckleberries Bob brought me. Now I pay horrendous prices for a gallon each summer.

We had lots of summer fun because we were one big family. Powell is where I met my first Forest Service wives who taught me everything about living in the woods. We seldom went to Missoula so planned all our meals ahead of time. Pies were easy enough to bake in a wood stove, but cakes and bread were tricky. We were able to call the Lolo store with a crank phone and they would send out groceries every Tuesday via the station truck. We had parties for any occasion and everybody came. Dads were prone to go up and get snow to make homemade ice cream for children's birthdays. Fishing trips meant fish fries and baseball games at Powell Campground. The grounds of the station were never watered or mowed so there were lots of wild flowers and migrating birds and sometimes grazing mules. There were few buildings in total. My how things change over time.

One special thing these wives, Vera, Barbara, Berle and Jane, did for Bob and I was to give us a big baby shower for our first son with plenty of Missoula people invited to the station. It was Memorial Day of

Pack string at Powell R.S., Clearwater National Forest.

1954. Memorial weekend was the time when families usually moved out to Powell. That year many people had to be pulled through a big mud hole (also coined Bob's mud hole) with a power wagon near the Shotgun Creek road takeoff.

Everyone seems to have one bear story. Bears often came later in the summer. A garbage bear usually had to be dispatched because they became repeaters and spent most of their time tearing up things at the station. Our story happened one September. A bear tore-up the Packers tent and raided our garbage can. Our dog would bark from under the trailer but would never give chase. Night after night Bob would tip toe to the door, revolver in hand, but as he slide the door the bear would take off – except one memorable night. The fellows were having an evening discussion on the office steps. The station phones weren't working and I was alone with our son. I heard the garbage can rattle, I slid the door back knowing that he would leave. He just looked at me, with wonder in his eyes. When Bob came home the bear was gone – one smart bear.

To this day the Lochsa River is my favorite place. I love the sound it makes from the early spring roar to the quiet ripple of the fall. What wonderful sounds to lull me to sleep at night.

ANTS – ANTS – ANTS
CLARKIA RANGER DISTRICT
by Lois Puckett

In 1955 the St. Joe was still a forest and Clarkia was still a ranger district. George Duvendack was Forest Supervisor and Oswald J. Esterl was the District Ranger. Jack was his Assistant. We lived in a little cottage back in the woods. We weren't exactly isolated but there was no one within shouting distance. Jack was in Wyoming on a fire, and I was awaiting the birth our of first daughter.

It was a dark and stormy night. I was alone and very pregnant. Lynne was past due. The summer had been hot and humid, in fact July and August were two of the most miserable months I have ever spent. I had not been sleeping very well and this particular evening there was a thunder storm with rain that cooled the air off so that it made sleep possible. I dozed off for a while only to be rudely awakened by a sharp bit on my leg. I moved and tried to get away but more bites followed so I turned on the light and saw a ribbon of ants coming over the edge of the bed, under the sheet toward my legs. With frantic brushing and slapping I cleared the bed and looked at the floor. A river of ants about a foot wide was coming through the bedroom door straight for the bed. I reached for a slipper and started beating ants. When the pile got too large I'd push them aside, roll over, change arms and wap some more. By the time both arms were tired and I couldn't reach any more so I put my slippers on and stomped to the bedroom door. The "river" crossed the living room and was coming in under the back door. They were carrying eggs and moving in out of the rain.

Now I could get to the phone and call for help! Except it's only 4:30 a.m. and Betty Esterl, the ranger's wife, would think the baby was coming. So I handled them myself. I stomped, wapped, and swept uncounted dustpans full of dead ants. They finally quit coming under the door, so I made coffee and called Betty after 7. She and Betty Ann, her daughter came over and commiserated with me. Our daughter finally arrived a week or so later after a mad dash to Moscow, but that's another story.

FOND MEMORIES
by Gene Covey

Seeley Lake, Montana, was where Bill started to work as a forester, and since there was no district housing available for us to rent, we rented the only place available in, or near, Seeley Lake. It was a privately owned twenty foot trailer with an addition built on. The addition had a sheepherder's stove. When we built a fire in it, the sides got red hot (really red), as it was a single piece of thin metal. So, Bill put a hardware cloth fence around it so that Mike (2 ½ years) and Carmel (3 months) would not be able to touch it. This trailer was located just a few miles from the station. Mike called it "The Shack."

The people who owned it were named "Swallow," and had a sign on the entry "Swallows Nest." So, the "Coveys" had moved into the "Swallows Nest." Something that Bill just reminded me of was that a skunk came into the yard and ran our cat up a tree. Thank goodness the wives on the station were great gals and would invite me for coffee a time or two a week, so that our children could play with their children. Helped my sanity, also!

In the fall a nice (?) man called on us and asked if we would rent his lakeshore house on the south end of the lake. We said, "No, as we wanted a year-around place and we were aware that he and his family used the house in the summer." He said, "No, they were not going to be using it anymore and wanted to rent it year around." O.K., we rented it in September. In June, he evicted us because they wanted it for the summer!!!!!!

The "Swallows Nest".

Thank goodness, the ranger, Tom Coston, allowed us to rent a small trailer (about 20 feet) on the administrative site. So, our children (then 1 and 3 years) slept in the bed and Bill and I slept on the sleeper couch. During the daytime, the children and I spent as much time as possible outside. It didn't take long to do my cleaning, so I did a lot of knitting and sewing, also. Of course, this was on the shore of the lake, and we spent a lot of time outside. The weather happened to be excellent that summer, so we really had a great time.

There, we frequently had a bear at the garbage can, but our trustworthy Golden Retriever would warn me, and I would make sure the children were inside until it left.

In the fall, the good news was that the Forest Service inherited two surplus, reject trailers from the Navy. One of them was about thirty-four feet, with two bedrooms. The district built on a room to accommodate a wood heating stove and washing machine. The temperature did get down to about 30 degrees below zero and the plumbing under the sink froze unless we kept the cupboard doors open.

In January Bill was transferred to Fenn Ranger Station on the Selway River in Idaho and we were delighted to have a two bedroom house, with a basement, and also a beautiful location. We thought it was great, but the children fussed for awhile because they had to leave their friends at Seeley.

After that, we always lived in or near towns, but I still have fond memories of our lives and the many close friends we had on ranger stations.

Now that both of our children are married and have children of their own, we all still enjoy going camping either at Seeley Lake or Fenn Ranger Station. And Mike gave one of his sons the middle name of "Fenn." So, apparently, they have fond memories, also.

MOVING – MOVING
by Kay Thompson

We all moved more times than we want to remember – but of the twenty-three (yes, 23) times we moved from 1949, when Keith graduated from Colorado State University until we moved to Anderson, Indiana, in 1989, I believe we made one of the quickest moves on record. And maybe one of the worst when we left Coeur d'Alene, Idaho, in October in 1989 in shirt sleeves and spent the night in Sheridan, Wyoming, with dozens of truckloads of bawling hungry and freezing cows because of a sudden blizzard that closed the highway. And we finished that move on December 18th when Indiana had 25 below zero and it was the lowest – EVER – on record, and they kept repeating that the windchill factor was 75 below!

The quickest move was from St. Maries, Idaho, to Yaak Ranger Station located between Bonners Ferry and Troy, Montana. Keith had been up there for two weeks and had been home for the weekend and gone back and would come home when we would move in about two weeks. Art Johnson, who was coming to take Keith's place and living in Bonners, called me with the news that they were planning to close the bridge at Bonners as soon as Tuesday. I made phone calls to the State Highway, the movers, to Keith, the office and phoned for a lot of help. The movers contacted the Highway Department and they promised not to close the bridge until Tuesday "evening" – whatever that meant. The moving company said they would be there at 8 a.m. and someone came and took my baby and two other kids; people from the office showed up and everyone was already packing experts so one did drapes and curtains and one did the kitchen. Someone called that I could not leave without a going away gift and party. Since I had no dishes and not even napkins they brought everything – it was very short – and I went back to work. Keith came home about midnight and I packed until 3 a.m. This move left our oldest son with no Sunday shoes and these were found four years later in a box I had dragged out of the St. Maries attic – saw the shoes – threw them in – and never needed whatever was in that box. When we did find them four years later they fit his little brother.

So the van came – we loaded – someone fed us – we left for Bonners Ferry and we stopped to eat and the moving van went by and OVER THE BRIDGE. When we came along later – I became very sick. Upon arrival kind ladies, Ruth Farbo and Elsie Eddy took my kids (Tom and Byron and the whole crew helped unload) and I crawled into bed. When someone brought a box and asked where to put it – LAST ON – FIRST OFF, it was some junk from the garage and I told them all that if it wasn't furniture to put it in the garage – which we were unable to use for a month or more. BUT we survived and many more moves after that. We made wonderful, lifetime friends everywhere.

Sylvanite Ranger Station, February 1957. Lots and lots of snow. Kay was reading late at night, and Keith was gone. She had this feeling that someone was watching her. Closed her book and walked into the hall, where there was a window. Sure enough, she was being watched – the snow was so deep that their dog "Sparkle" was looking in the window at her!

FOREST SERVICE PEOPLE ARE THE BEST
by Ruth Freeman

In May of 1959, Jim was offered the ranger's position at Slate Creek R.S. on the Nezperce National Forest – a brand new station. It was the first time that Jim didn't ask me whether we should make the move! We loved being on the Salmon River and had watched the new station building process and dreamed of what it would be like to live there.

The new station was built on five acres of land between White Bird and Riggins, Idaho. It consisted of three modern residences with attached garages, a shop/garage, and office/warehouse. Highway 95 bordered the back side of the station, today the highway has been relocated and runs parallel with the Salmon River in front of the ranger station. We had never lived in a new house before; three bedrooms, a bathroom with a shower and tub, a living room with large picture windows and a fireplace, a kitchen with modern appliances and an eating area. A full basement with an oil furnace for heat. A far cry from our first ranger station (Castle Creek R.S.) – no electricity, learning to cook on a big old wood stove, besides heating with wood, a wash board for doing laundry, and the creek for our ice box. The Salmon River climate was ideal for having a garden and the neighbors had fruit trees that grew more then they could use. I canned one day and froze produce the next day. We could see the snow line on the mountains across the river, but we were living in the sun belt. Our cup runneth over!!

Jim had gone off to the woods to check a timber sale and would be gone overnight. Jane and Jimmy left for school in Riggins on the school bus. Their bus driver came from Riggins each morning so he knew of any road hazards before beginning the route. (In later years he became the Idaho county sheriff – Gene Fuzzell.) An interesting aspect of going to school in Riggins is that it is in the Mountain Time Zone, the Salmon River being the dividing line. Slate Creek R.S. is in Pacific Time Zone. Many the time the question came up "whose time?" After sending people off in various directions I was staring at a bushel of pears and peaches to can. We were expecting a baby in the fall, and I just didn't feel that great. Dorothea Miner and Donna Lindsey lived in the other two residences, and they said they'd watch Jill and Jody Kay if I wanted to go see the doctor. I drove up the White Bird Hill with its numerous switchbacks and sat in the doctor's office waiting room in Grangeville. Hoping a shot in the arm would nip whatever bug I was coming down with. Imagine my surprise when Dr. Buttermore told me I was going across the street to the hospital and have my baby! I exclaimed, "I can't have a baby now. Jim's not home and the kids are in school." Dr. Buttermore explained to me that I didn't have a choice. He also eased my mind saying he was going fishing on the Salmon River after my delivery and he'd stop in at the ranger station and give them the news!

JacLyn was born at 12:34 p.m. and Dr. Buttermore still had the better part of the day for fishing. Someone from the supervisor's office came and picked up our station wagon and took it to the F.S. vehicle compound. That still left telling Jim. The solution was to fly the patrol plane in the general area Jim was working and hope to spot his F.S. pickup. When the plane showed up one of the fellows on the ground told the others, "I think that plane is looking for someone." Jim continued what he was doing but said, "wave your arms and they'll see you." Next thing they know a bag of nails is dropped with a note, asking "is Jim Freeman there?" They waved their arms again. Another bag of nails with the message, "you're a Dad again, report to Grangeville."

Jim had to wait until evening because the road was closed and a line of logging trucks and equipment were ahead of him. When he did arrive at the hospital he was refused admittance at first – he looked like he could contaminate the hospital with his muddy logging boots and tin pants, hard hat and wool shirt, plus a large black and while collie type dog in tow!

Dorothea and Donna met the kids as they got off the school bus and watched everyone until Jim got home later that night. They even canned the peaches and pears!

JacLyn, 6-months-old,
in her TeeterBabe.

Slate Creek R.S. has always been one of my favorite places to live. Several years later in November when we moved to Kalispell, Montana, our rose bushes were still blooming. That evening when we stopped in Libby for supper, Jane's lizard froze – in just the time it took for us to eat. Thus the start of another adventure!

There is nothing like being a part of the big F. S. family. The best people in the world are the friends we have made in our career with the Forest Service. In all our moves – 14 of them – we were never a stranger. There was always someone who knew someone we knew, and you immediately had a bonding.

Twelve switchbacks on the old White Bird Hill (the hill's hairpin curves have made memorable impressions on Highway 93 travelers.)

Ranger's dwelling – 1960. Slate Creek Ranger Station, Nezperce National Forest.

Jim Freeman – 1961.

SORT OF A BEAR STORY
by Betty Cloninger
(Mrs. Russ Cloninger)

It was 1959. Oh my! That was forty years ago! Our husbands were out in the field on Forest Service business, so Betty Robe and I decided to go camping. We wanted to go to Glacier Park and hike up to Grinnell Glacier. We loaded up my station wagon with grub box, ice chest, sleeping bags and, most importantly, fish poles. We did go to Grinnell Glacier, took the two boat trips to get to the top of the glacier. The night of August 17, we had cooked our trout over the campfire, cleaned up camp, and headed for the sack – our sleeping bags in the back of the station wagon. We had seen a big black bear near our camp earlier in the evening, so we had put our ice chest and fish poles on top of the car, just in case.

About 11:30 in the night, our car began shaking violently. THE BEAR! THE BEAR! I crawled over the front seat, turned on the headlights, honked the horn furiously, and looked all around. No bear! So, nervously, I crawled back into my sleeping bag. It wasn't until the next morning that word finally arrived at Park Headquarters that what had shaken us so violently was an earthquake. It was actually one of the most severe earthquakes ever recorded on the North American continent. Several hundred miles to the south of us, near Yellowstone Park, the quake had shaken a 7,000 foot mountain so hard that it had fallen into the Madison River. Well, it was only half of the mountain. But that was no bear! Of the nearly 300 people camped in the canyon near Hebgen Dam that night, 28 people were killed, and 19 of them are still buried under the slide. If you visit there today, you will find Quake Lake, which was formed by the slide that dammed up the Madison River in its narrow canyon. Quake Lake and the Madison River are again a favorite fishing and camping site and tourist attraction. But on my trip to Montana last year, I took another look at that huge scar of rock, where half the mountain fell in. And I made a vow. You would never fine ME camped under the other half of that mountain.

SEX, VIOLENCE AND DEATH
IN DARKEST DESCANSO
by Donna D. Heilman

In 1959 my husband, Ed Heilman, was District Ranger on the Descanso District of the Cleveland National Forest in Southern California. We were living on the Ranger Station in what seemed to us a veritable palace: three bedrooms with a formal dining room, a big living room with a fireplace, and windows all around that made the house sunny and open to the lovely view. The house was on a slight hill with huge oak trees on three sides and a lawn in front stretching down to the driveway and the Ranger Station office, a veritable oasis in the midst of the hot, dry semi-desert of eastern San Diego county.

But in this almost idyllic scene not all was as peaceful as it appeared. People in the village of Descanso, a number of whom were my friends, began receiving obscene phone calls. The caller always knew the name of the person who answered the phone, even when it was a child, and when the person would ask "who is this?" he would reply "Joe." Needless to say, this had everyone quite on edge. The whole community numbered only a few hundred people, and everyone was at least somewhat acquainted with everyone else; so we all began to look uneasily at all the men wondering if he was the caller. We parents had to warn our children not to accept a ride from, nor to be along with, anyone, not even a friend, because no one knew who the caller was and what he might do given the chance.

One day Sylvia, a friend of mine, called me. She was terribly upset because a woman who lived in San Diego had called her and said that she had gotten an obscene phone call from a man who identified himself as Joe Barker who lived in Descanso. That was, indeed the name of Sylvia's husband. Joe was questionable in some ways, having a quirk that I found very off-putting. I saw him occasionally when I was visiting Sylvia because his rather irregular work schedule often allowed him to be home on weekdays. This odd quirk consisted in what seemed to be an inordinate interest in sex, and I found it really amusing to note how long it took after a conversation began before he managed to bring the subject around to that topic. However, he was quite well read on a wide variety of subjects; so I simply changed the subject and then enjoyed talking with him. In light of all this, when Sylvia told me about the woman's call it certainly aroused my suspicions. Joe worked at a Naval Air Station near San Diego and could easily have made calls from there to the surrounding towns.

Nonetheless I soothed her as best I could, saying that no one would make a call like that and then identify himself, that there had to be some mistake. I didn't tell anyone else about this development, but of course it added further to my unease.

The Ranger Station was the only symbol of law enforcement in the Descanso Valley; so people were very likely to come to the office, or to our house if the office was closed, in case of an emergency. One Sunday when we were still very on edge because of these obscene calls a man drove up to the station and told Ed that he had been to the home-office of a real estate woman named Mabel Muntean, who lived a mile or two out of town. He said the door was open, and he could see through the screen what appeared to be a woman's body. Ed called the Deputy Sheriff, Ralph Nunnery, who lived in Pine Valley about ten miles up the road. Together they went to Mrs. Muntean's house, where they found the room a shambles, blood splattered all over the floor and walls, and her mutilated body lying in the midst of this ghastly scene. Since she was a business woman it was supposed that she kept money there from time to time; so maybe the murderer had been after that. There was no sign of forcible entry; so it appeared that her murderer had been know to Mrs. Muntean, that she had let him or her into the house. That suggested that it could have been a local, someone in Descanso, perhaps someone we knew. Now we were really frightened; obscene phone calls by someone in the town, and now violent murder by someone who seemed to be known to the victim.

All of a sudden our house felt huge and vulnerable, and all those windows, which had opened to the sunlight and the beautiful view, became black holes through which an intruder could watch me. We had no shades on the windows, and Ed spent most evenings working at the office; so after putting the children to bed I sat alone in that seemingly vast, silent house surrounded by the threatening darkness.

At this point Ed insisted that we buy a gun; so we went to San Diego and bought a .22 caliber pistol, and from then on for several weeks we went out into the open country and I had to practice shooting. I was afraid of the gun and hated the noise and the smell, but a least I could have brandished the thing and maybe scared off an attacker.

The sheriff's department questioned people who had known Mrs. Muntean or worked for her or had any business with her, but after a month or so they had no firm suspect. Then they got a call from the emergency room of a nearby hospital that a young man from one of the Indian Reservations east of San Diego had been brought in suffering from acute alcoholism. In his delirium he kept crying out "Blood! Blood!" over and over again. The young man died before the deputies got there; but when they did, they recognized him as someone they had questioned earlier because he was known to have worked for Mrs. Muntean doing gardening and other odd jobs. There was never any proof that he had committed the crime, but no other likely suspect was found either, and the Sheriff's Department concluded that he was probably the murderer and just before he died and cried out in guilt and horror at what he had done.

As for the obscene phone calls, they seemed to stop at about this same time, and a few days later I again visited Sylvia, and Joe was there. After a few minutes conversation he began to tell me about a visit he had received from a couple of sheriff's deputies while he was at work. It seems that they never accused him of making the calls, they simply chatted about them in a very pleasant way. Then Joe smiled at me in a pleased, sort to triumphant way. I can only conclude that he had made the calls, found it exciting to come as close as he possibly could to getting caught, and found it very satisfying to have gotten away with it. Not unlike a bungee jumper or hang glider or other thrill seeker, he had wanted to see how close he could come to disaster and still come through unscathed.

After all this, things quieted down, except for the young forester who was found tramping through the woods in nearby Mt. Laguna, naked except for his boots and socks. But that's another story.

Note: "Sylvia and Joe Barker" are fictitious names for real people; all the other names are real ones.

ON THEIR OWN, BABY AND MOM
MOVE TO THE UPPER FORD, YAAK, MONTANA
by Jean Johnson

From San Antonio, Texas, to Rexford, Montana, in less than a month. It was May 1959 and Dal received his discharge in April of 1959. This was his new assignment as he had worked for the F.S. before being drafted in April of 1957. This is the old Rexford that is now under Lake Koocanusa. We were fortunate enough to have housing provided at the ranger station. This would not be a permanent place of living as the station was moving to a new complex in Eureka. Rexford was being dismantled as the Libby dam would create a reservoir that would cover the site. Imagine my excitement along with Ruth Kern, the ranger's wife and Carol Sedlacek, the assistant ranger's wife. We were going to be choosing countertops, tile, linoleum, and colors for the house we would live in. On top of that, a couple of months later I found that we would be expecting our first child in June of 1960. We all moved into our homes that fall of 1959. Not enough furniture to furnish the house, but that didn't matter. The essentials were there.

May 1960 Dal came home and said, "guess what?" They want me to be one of the assistant rangers on the Sylvanite Ranger District." We would live at the Upper Ford which is 25 miles north of Sylvanite. The Yaak is beautiful country, but it had dirt roads that muddied up in the spring and were near impassable in winter until the snow plow showed. We would be approximately 45 miles from Libby if the South Fork was kept open in the winter by J. Neils Lumber company, otherwise it was a 60 mile trip. No electricity, no phone service from Upper Ford to Sylvanite and then not in winter when lines were down, and having to go outside to start a pump, hopefully, to have water was what we had awaiting us. Eureka is 65 miles from Kalispell and that was the nearest hospital. Our baby was due about June 17th, but like many babies did not arrive until ready. Meanwhile, Dal had to report for work at Upper Ford while I stayed in Eureka. The 17th came and went and no baby. Dal come home on Friday nights and stayed until Sunday. He came home Friday the 24th and we had a spicy supper then afterwards went to see the "Horse Soldiers" with John Wayne at the local theater. Toward the end of the movie I was beginning to feel uncomfortable and put it down to our spicy supper. We went home and stayed up till midnight, then went to bed. I awoke about 1:30 and was really feeling uncomfortable and it dawned on me that I was having labor pains. Waking Dal, we left for Kalispell arriving about 4:30 a.m. Now I really was having pains and Dal was getting worried. We made it okay but not by much as our baby girl, who we named Jodi, arrived around 5:20 a.m.

Dal had made arrangements with a private moving company out of Missoula to move us to the Yaak. The deal was that Dal would help load and unload the truck and therefore only one person would bring the truck. It sounded good at the time, but we had a fire bust and Dal had to leave Sunday afternoon the 26th for the Yaak. The mover was coming that Wednesday and Dal was unable to be there to help. So, with new baby in hand and movers coming, I took apart the kitchen table, disconnected the washer and dryer and other furniture as required, such as bed, crib, etc. No way was I going to be able to help load the truck especially with a freezer, hide-a-bed and other heavy furniture. Ranger

Chuck Kern had a couple of men or college students on standby at the station and he sent them over to help load. I didn't have enough time to clean the house so gave Ruth Kern money to hire a gal to come in and clean it.

I was pooped and it was late when we left Eureka. We, including the mover, went via Troy as Al and Lucille Gibson lived there and we told them they could use our freezer as it would not be usable in the Yaak and we didn't want to store it. I was so glad to see Lucille. The Gibsons have four children and she was a great comfort to me during this trying time. I stayed overnight with them and the mover stayed in Troy.

Back in those days we didn't have the car seats and belts like we have today. Being as I was driving by myself I couldn't hold Jodi. She traveled to the Yaak in an encyclopedia box that at one time held part of a Britannica encyclopedia set. We still have the encyclopedias and the boxes they came in. I put padding in the bottom and a blanket and wrapped her up and she fit snugly in the box. Of course, I didn't put the lid on the box. When we arrived at the Upper Ford, I was in a quandary on how the truck would get unloaded. Imagine my relief when I found there were two college boys on standby in the Upper Ford office. One of them was Steve Smart, son of Bob and Frances Smart. Bob was the ranger at Troy when Dal fresh out of college came to Troy as a Junior Forester. These two guys helped our mover unload the truck and

Upper Ford on the Yaak, Sylvanite Ranger District.

everything was piled in the living room. The Upper Ford house is a log house with a bedroom, an open room and bath upstairs. The downstairs is the living room and kitchen with a porch off the living room and a small porch off the kitchen.

For the next two weeks, Jodi and I lived in the living room and kitchen. I slept on the hide-a-bed without pulling it out and she slept in her encyclopedia box. I was able to get into some of the boxes that had our clothes in them. Enough pots and dishes were found so I could cook. All I had to cook on was a wood range and my washing machine was a scrub board. A few of the diapers ended with holes until I got the knack on how to use the board. Our lights were a Coleman lantern and kerosene lamps. This didn't bother me as my folks had had a cabin on Flathead Lake and no electricity. I was used to lighting and taking care of these type of lanterns. Getting the woodstove to burn correctly was another matter. We had a wood cookstove at the Flathead cabin but I didn't cook on it. I must admit I burned a few things before figuring out how to control it. We had a kerosene refrigerator that had a very small freezing unit. We didn't keep frozen food while in the Yaak because of lack of room. As I recall, the refrigerator was working when I arrived. Dal probably was using it during the weekdays he was staying and so I didn't have to deal with starting it.

Our closest neighbor was 1/4 mile. She and several others in the

Jodi with Dal's bear – 1961.

Upper Yaak came to meet us and get acquainted. Knowing the boys were close by gave some comfort in case I had an emergency. Before leaving Troy, I had stopped at the grocery store to load up as it was too far to drive on dusty dirt roads for bread, milk, etc. During our stay in the Yaak, I baked all our bread and other goods such as cookies, cake, etc.

We used dry milk and canned milk. Later when the girls were old enough to drink it, we bought raw milk from a local family. It was heavy with cream and many a spring day found Dad cranking the ice cream freezer. Fresh meat was eaten when we went to town and the first few days after getting home. We went to town once a month. Dal caught fish in the Yaak. We ate canned meat and had an above ground root cellar that we could store some vegetables and canned goods. We planted a garden and put a fence around it to keep out the deer. The only thing about it all was the elevation was so high and growing season too short to grow anything worthwhile. Out by the old woodshed, someone had planted rhubarb. We used it when it was ready in the spring. The Yaak is great huckleberry country. Many a gallon did we pick while living there. Was I glad to see Dal when he finally got off the fires. We were able to arrange the furniture, put the house in good order and make a home for ourselves. Of all the places we've lived, this was by far our favorite. We were there for four years and had one more baby, a girl, Jana, during that time. I don't want to write a book, but I could go on and on about other stories and adventures we had while living in the Yaak. That will have to wait until another time as the many other adventures we had when Dal was sent to Red River, Idaho, as the ranger following his Yaak assignment.

A SNAKEY START
by Betty Filius

I came to Montana from Michigan on the old Milwaukee Railroad in early 1961 to teach at Sentinel High School in Missoula. That career was cut short when Dave and I were married a few months later at St. Paul's Methodist Church in Helena. Dave had been working for the Forest Service since the previous spring and his main job was as a forester on the Canyon Ferry Ranger District of the Helena National Forest with responsibility for the district timber sale program.

Late that summer Dave was playing catch-up after a busy season of smoke chasing, so he asked me one day if I would come along with him and help tally as he paint marked a small timber sale up Spring Creek, a short tributary off White's Gulch.

The proposed sale contained a nice patch of Douglas fir trees for which someone had requested a small sales permit to harvest. While Dave ranged up and down the slopes with his tree marking paint gun, diameter tape and Abney level, I followed along in the dry drainage bottom, marking down the tree species and measurement on a cruise sheet in an aluminum tatum folder as he called out the numbers.

Since we lived in a small upstairs apartment in Helena and I was by this time several months pregnant, I appreciated the chance to get out of town and see what kind of work he did day after day in the woods. He'd been gone a lot that summer, sometimes for a week or more at a time, and I was enjoying the outing – until a big thick three foot long tan colored snake slithered past my feet.

I yelled up to Dave that I had a big snake down here with me and he asked what kind it was. By that time I had noticed a set of rattles on it and had relayed that information in a decidedly more anxious tone. Dave yelled back for me to stand still, and came on the run.

When Dave got there the rattler was starting to move away. Dave was impressed that I had not gone completely into orbit, but having been a biology teacher and a farm girl, I wasn't one to get too alarmed at animals. Still in all, it was the first rattlesnake for both of us. We decided to leave it alone, but for visibility, Dave painted it up with a full length coat of yellow tree paint and it slithered on its way.

That was the one and only trip to the woods that I ever had on Dave's official time for the next thirty years, until as a signed-up volunteer, I got to accompany Dave and the head of the Norwegian Forest Service and his wife on a float plane ride over the Boundary Waters. The snake adventure was however, one of the first of many fond memories I had as a Forest Service wife.

IN AND OUT STATIONS
by Sue (Crupper)Blunn

I have been associated with the Forest Service almost my entire life, first as a daughter, then a wife and now as an employee. It's been a good life with lots of fun times, good friends and many experiences.

The first two stations where I lived with my parents, John and

Lucy Crupper, were Ft. Howe R.S. on the Custer N.F. and the F.S. nursery at Hayes, Kansas. In 1946, we then moved to the Nezperce N. F. at Grangeville, Idaho. We were here for four years until my Father went to California for his Master's Degree. We then returned to Grangeville where he became District Ranger at Adams R.S. which was an in and out station. From there we moved to St. Regis, Montana, which ended my in and out ranger station living for a while.

When my husband, Tom, received his forestry degree I once again started living at in and out stations. Our first station was Shoshone Work Center on the Wallace R.S. on the Coeur d'Alene N. F. This is where we became really acquainted with the bears. Each evening they would visit the cookhouse and then come by our house on their way to the dump. One evening while playing cards in our living room we looked up to see a bear watching us through the door.

After living here three summers, and a month after our older daughter, Sheryl, was born, we moved 50 miles back into the woods to Magee Ranger Station. We also had bears here but they weren't quite as entertaining.

There were several couples and families there during the summer and we had a lot of good times the three years we were there. I remember our Friday night "happy hours" with Art and Mary Olson. We had to drive

Our house – 1962. Magee Ranger Station, Coeur d'Alene National Forest. Shoveling snow off roof.

across a one-lane bridge on the way back to our house and sometimes it wouldn't hold still after our "happy hours." It would also be hard to forget sitting in the dark each evening in our house. If we turned on a light, the house filled up with those tiny "noseeums" and we became their feast.

The real experience, though, was the twice a month trip to town for groceries and everything else. Once Tom moved out in the spring, he didn't have any great desire to spend weekends traveling to Couer d'Alene. Sheryl and I would drive in on a Friday to shop and one summer another wife and her two children joined us. We had a Chevy Corvair at the time with the trunk in the front and a back seat that folded down. I don't know how we fit five people and all our groceries in this car, but we did. We'd get an early start because it would take about two hours to drive the 50 miles over forest roads. We arrived in town and started our shopping – to the drug store, the library, sometimes a doctor appointment, then lunch and finally the grocery store. We didn't want to forget anything because there wasn't a store around the corner at Magee. Then we would stop at Fernan, pick up the mail and call to let Tom know we were heading home.

Tom, Sue and Sheryl Blunn,
Magee Ranger Station – 1962.

One Friday on our way back to Magee, we met another car (one of the summer employees headed to town) on a corner and collided. No one injured, but with the groceries in the front of the car, we had a mess. I can still see cottage cheese scattered all over the place. After that I made the grocery run to town on Thursdays.

Looking back now, I wonder how we did these trips, but at the time it was no big deal. It did become more difficult after our second daughter, Gretchen, was born, but I think I only made one more trip. We were transferred that summer (1964) to a year round station.

We became very adept at packing our household items since we moved twice a year from 1959-1964. We could pack everything in one day and unpack it all the next day. In November of 1963, we broke all previous records. We were still at Magee, I was eight months pregnant and it started snowing. Tom became a bit concerned and called the movers that afternoon. They said they could be out the next morning so we packed everything that evening. No problem! It was a different story when we moved to Missoula in 1990 after Tom retired. It had been several years since we had moved and the packing and unpacking was much more traumatic.

MISSOULA, MONTANA, TO JUNEAU, ALASKA
December 1962
by Lucy Crupper

We moved many times during John's 30-plus years with the Forest Service. The most memorable for me was the one from Missoula, Montana, to Juneau, Alaska, in December 1962. Alaska had interested us for a long time, so, when the offer came, the answer was, "Yes."

Arrangements were made for us to ride on a new Alaska ferry due to sail at a convenient time because I did not want to fly. Since nothing in life is perfect, the ferry did not meet the maiden voyage schedule and our time ran out. So, on December 7, we put the final items in the car and pointed it north.

We visited our family at Hayden Lake and with their help repacked the car, which was badly over-loaded. Several cardboard cartons and a spare tire were mailed to Juneau. (Postal officials were very relieved when we arrived many days later to pick them up – especially the tire.)

Reluctant good-byes and business in Spokane took a chunk of time out of this day, and we traveled only to Omak, Washington. Since dense fog had moved in, that was far enough.

People warned us that the farther we went up the Alaska Highway the colder it would get, and to plan our wardrobes accordingly. Good advice, but strangely unnecessary. Contrary to expectation, we were blessed with fine weather. Early one morning as we headed up the road, a beautiful, bright moon was shining in the rear window of the car, and each day we had rare opportunities to observe the thermal belt and enjoy the spectacular area through which we traveled.

Rain came on the last day as we reached Whitehorse, Yukon Territory. Tickets to Skagway, Alaska, were waiting at the White Pass Railroad Station, which in 1962 carried both passengers and freight. Our motel was near, we checked in, freshened up and, despite the rain, ate

ALASKA HIGHWAY
DAWSON CREEK — 918M.
To WHITEHORSE

MISSOULA, MT. — 2175M
To WHITEHORSE

PACIFIC OCEAN

RAIL WHITEHORSE
SKAGWAY TESLIN
JUNEAU WATSON LAKE

ROCKY MOUNTAINS

MUNCHO LAKE
FORT NELSON

WONOWON

FORT ST. JOHN
DAWSON CREEK MILE ZERO

To PRINCE GEORGE

Sketched map of Alaska Highway from mile 0 to Whitehorse, rail to Skagway and plane to Juneau.

dinner and saw as much as we could of this exciting city near the head of the Yukon River. Next morning the temperature started to drop, the rain turned to ice, and the highway was closed for two days.

The train was ready early the next morning and as we took our seats we could see our car on a section ahead of ours where it re-appeared on every curve. The train ride is truly an event. The route cuts through breath-taking scenery, Robert Service country, and is rife with Gold Rush history.

Lunch at Lake Bennett is a great treat with a family style meal served in a logging camp atmosphere. Time is planned only for eating so extra-curricular activities may cause you to miss some of the menu items. It's wise to eat quickly, taste everything and not ask about unfamiliar delicacies. Just eat and enjoy.

Skagway looked both exciting and formidable as we pulled into the depot. The setting is very beautiful, lying at the water's edge with a backdrop of high mountains; typical of the cities in southeast Alaska. Lights twinkled in the black dark of a December afternoon relieved by a light blanket of snow.

While the rain turned the snow to slush, a pleasant customs officer cleared us for entry, helped John get some things out of the car, rearrange the load, and directed us to a garage where we could store the car. We had literally "missed the boat" by one day that would have taken the car to Juneau. The manager of the garage accepted our keys and all the worldly goods carefully selected to use until we were settled. He assured us he would get it on the next boat and he did – in a month. A warm, dry motel not far away was a welcome sight.

Later at dinner I committed my first *cheechako* blunder. A basketball flyer advertised a game and I said to John, "If we don't fly out tomorrow we can go to the game." The long suffering waitress looked at me and said, "Honey, if you can't get out, they can't get in." It was now that we learned no planes had come in for five days.

Next morning the plane arrived and we were quickly driven to the airport in the pouring rain. We boarded and I could see the seats 2 by 2 on both sides of the aisle. The rain like a deluge? The seats 2 by 2? I had a fleeting thought of the Ark. "Regulars" occupied the window seats so we could not sit together.

I found a seat and fumbled around trying to figure out how to put my seat belt on as the pilot hurried down the aisle, hesitated beside me to say, "Lady, get your seat belt fastened." By now I am as nervous as the proverbial cat and, without thinking, blurted out, "I've never flown before and I'm doing it as fast as I can." He stopped in his tracks, turned around (as did all the passengers on the plane), instructed me in my role as a passenger, delivered an air-sick bag, walked back to the cockpit door, turned once more and said, "Lady, you sure picked yourself some plane and some day to start flying." So be it.

We stopped briefly at Haines and in that short time a health nurse said, "Oh, if I had known I would have given you some dramamine," and an old-timer muttered, "You shouldn't have eaten breakfast." So much for a condemned person getting a last meal. Now the plane is full and it's almost as wet inside as outside with small puddles on the floor sloshing around with every move. On to Juneau.

We now fly low over the choppy waters famous for freezing temperatures. The trees grow down to the water's edge and mountains disappear in the clouds and fog. We go right past the Juneau airport; no one is going to the South 48 today. Oh?

Continuing down the Lynn Canal we fly lower and lower, losing most of what little altitude we had. There was a quick glimpse of Mendenhall Glacier. Ahead we see the Juneau-Douglas bridge; Juneau on one side of the water and Douglas across on the opposite side. Surely we are going to hit that bridge. No. Before I could catch my breath we flew under it and in seconds we splashed down. Water rushed up over the

Alaska Highway between mile 422 and 442, typical scenery.

windshield and all the side windows, ran off, and a man jumped out on the wing to secure the plane at the dock.

Oh, yes, this is the plane that lands on both land or water and this is the downtown part of Juneau. There is a bustle of passengers eager to get off and I am happy to join them.

The smiling faces were there to welcome us and take us to lunch. I wasn't too sure about lunch but good old Mother Earth felt great under my feet. Lunch was both fun and delicious.

Through the years we met wonderful, interesting people and made many friends. I loved the Forest Service life and wouldn't trade those years for anything else.

SHOSHONE CAMP
AND THE FORESTER VS. THE BEAR
by Jodi Hodge

May 1, 1963

Dear Friends,

> Dick and Jodi Hodge
> Shoshone Work Center
> Wallace Ranger Station
> Wallace, Idaho

The above address is to be our new mailing address. Our duplex address in Coeur d'Alene (CDA) will be history by the time you read this. My last day at the Doctor's Clinic was the end of April. They decorated a cake with me being treed by a bear. We'll see.

Our adventure in the forest next to the CDA River will start tomorrow. The Forest Service is renting us a place to live in the summer. It is a 1942 Army Communications trailer transported from the Kingston Ranger Station to a site at Shoshone next to the other residence. In the fall before winter snows we will need to rent housing in town. We will store all our extra household items for awhile.

I will continue to drive to CDA for doctor appointments as we are expecting the end of August or first of September. It will be about a hour and a half drive, but will give me a chance to town shop once a month!

Shoshone Center itself has an old office building, the cookhouse, a bunkhouse, some warehouses, and housing now for two families. Our neighbors, Don and Diane Pederson and four children, are living in the house that is next to our trailer.

Please write often. We will enjoy the news. There's one tv at the cookhouse, but the reception is poor. There aren't any phones in the homes so use Dick's work number if the need arises.

Our best,
Dick and Jodi

And that was the beginning of my Forest Service experiences. Dick had actually started his career with the Forest Service in St. Regis before we were married. After our September wedding, we both had jobs in CDA and lived there for nine months. However, we didn't really feel initiated into being "Forest Service" until the transfer to Shoshone.

My first trip to Shoshone was actually in April. Dick announced one evening we were being transferred. The following weekend we took a scouting trip to our new home. It was raining that Saturday morning. The dirt gravel road was muddy and seemed to go on forever. Finally, we were there. The old green trailer sat there with it's additions on each end, needing paint, a leveling job and lots of TLC to be a home. I started crying. Dick suggested we go meet the Pederson family and Diane invited us in for just baked chocolate chip cookies. That was the only bright spot I can remember in that day.

Moving day came all too soon and we became part of the Forest Service family at Shoshone Center that summer. Dick was the Forester in charge of Shoshone Camp. I kept busy giving our home the TLC it needed and helping Dick type descriptions of timber sales. I was anxious for things to do so using the old wringer washer and line drying clothes on Monday morning was fun. Ollie, the cook, always had coffee and treats available. Weekends usually meant a trip to town so during the week it was best to stay home. Going to one GS5 salary did not allow for extras. My trips to CDA for doctor appointments was the exception.

Evenings were spent at the cookhouse with Ollie and her assistants and a few F.S. guys. Extra desserts were always available to us. The choice of TV stations was not. The only one that came in was more snow than picture, was more frustrating than enjoyable. The river was cool and inviting and often in the afternoons wading helped to cool things off. We shared lots of Friday night meals with the Pedersons especially before pay days.

Another form of entertainment was going to visit the bears at the dump in the evenings. One time, however, the bear came to visit us instead. He woke us up by knocking very loudly on our door. There was only one door to the trailer. It was the entrance and the exit. Dick went out to investigate and the door window let him see eye to eye with our guest. No phones and one door – what now?

It was not going to be easy to persuade him to leave because that one door was located on a small porch which had a screen door that opened easily to let things in, but required a pull on the handle to allow it to swing open to let things out. Mr. Bear was an unhappy prisoner. He was rearranging everything on the porch. Would that door with the glass window be his next object of attention? How were we going to get him off the porch?

Dick came up with a possible solution to the problem. He would take out a bedroom window, climb out onto the roof, put a broom handle into the screen door handle, and open the door! The window comes out easily and Dick is ready for the ascent to the roof when, WHOOP-WHOOP. The bear solves the problem his way. He opens the screen door by hitting it so hard it flies off the hinges. The bear is happy to be free and so are we.

The window is replaced and we go back to bed. Daylight comes and I woke up with a case of the measles? Nope. More uninvited guests showed up while we were occupied with the bear. Noseeum bites are everywhere the covers were not. They apparently only liked girls because

Trailer with "bear" porch.

Dick escaped without any bites.

Our son, Scott, was born September 8th at CDA General Hospital at the end of the first summer at Shoshone. He had his first birthday party in the Army trailer. We moved to Shoshone for two more summers after spending the winters in Wallace and Kellogg.

The days at Shoshone seem long ago and so they were. We didn't know then they were a part of the past we would come to tell fond tales about. Stations where you moved in and out depending on the weather were unique and fun in their own ways. It was not so hard to move often when your possessions were few and your energies many. One of our winters was spent in Wallace and one in Kellogg. The third summer we lived in the trailer ended with our move to the Priest Lake Ranger Station and that's a story for another time.

NOT EXACTLY SANTA CLAUS COMES TO ...
COFFEE CREEK ?
by Donna D. Heilman

In the 1960's my husband, Ed Heilman, was the fire staff officer on the Forest Supervisor's staff of the Shasta-Trinity National Forests at Redding, California. We had a pleasant house at Redding, our kids were about 8 and 10 years old, Ed enjoyed the job, and it was a good time for us.

In December of maybe 1963 or 1964, there were heavy snows in the mountains of Northern California, but just before Christmas there was a sudden warm spell, heavy rains, and therefore serious flooding, particularly in the Trinity River area northwest of Redding. Many roads, bridges, and some buildings were washed out. Power and telephone lines were down, and many people had been isolated without power for several days at a time. Without power, freezers defrosted, water system pumps wouldn't work, and there was no relief in sight − not the situation that would make for a Merry Christmas for these flood victims.

Included among those isolated were the Coffee Creek Ranger Station people − the ranger, assistants, their families; and also some ranchers, loggers, and other area residents north of the Coffee Creek bridge, which had washed out. Coffee Creek is a fairly large drainage, about the size of Lolo Creek near Missoula. Since Trinity County agencies couldn't help at that time and place, any help would probably have to come from the Forest Service. Forest Supervisor Paul Stathem authorized a mission to take several electrical generators and other emergency equipment from the Redding Fire Cache to the Coffee Creek area, to refreeze freezers and otherwise provide some relief.

On Christmas Day another man from the Supervisor's staff drove a truck to be left with several generators at the accessible end of the Coffee Creek crossing, and Ed drove another vehicle to bring the truck driver back to Redding, even though both men were using up year-end annual leave. Ed invited me to ride along (this was acceptable back in those days). I arranged for our kids to stay with neighbors and we left on what was expected to be about a 4 or 5 hour round trip.

As it turned out, there were still some snowy patches and numerous trees down across the roads, so it took more than 4 hours just to get to where we were to leave the generators. It was almost dark by then, and it was raining steadily. There was a small grocery store/bar at the accessible end of the washed out bridge, and a small group of locals were there, some of whom had apparently been at the bar for some time. Outside were several trucks, some front-end loaders, and a big, beat-up old logging bulldozer (I learned later it was a Caterpillar D-8).

Ed and the other F.S. man knew several of the locals. After a few minutes of explanation of why we were there, the owner of the D-8, a really rough-hewn logger who couldn't speak a sentence without several swear words, volunteered to take the generators, tied down on the hood of his D-8, across the flooding Coffee Creek to the people on the other side.

By this time it was dark. With a few swear words thrown in for good measure, the logger asked me if I'd like to ride across the creek on the D-8 - just for the fun of it. He'd been across the XXQ#**# creek several times earlier in the YYZX## day, and it wasn't a MM###** problem. I was somewhat more adventuresome in those days, so I said yes, I'd like to ride over and back on the D-8. Ed had known this logger for several years and considered him more or less reliable, so Ed didn't try to stop me. So, with generators secured on the hood, I sat on top of the big winch at the rear of the operator's seat, held as best I could to the safety canopy, and away we went down into the rushing water.

Some of the trucks had their headlights aimed across Coffee Creek, and we could see whole trees, logs, and other debris rushing past in the really swift current. The rushing water made a lot of noise – in addition to the diesel engine of the D-8. Before we were very far into the creek, the water was well above the top of the tracks, and I was beginning to wonder just what I'd gotten into. Light from the truck lights behind us faded away. It was really dark. We couldn't see across the creek to the far bank.

Somewhere out in midstream the Cat got hung up on a big boulder in the streambed. It seemed to me the logger's movements with the controls showed that he was concerned that we might really be stuck. At this point I was trying to figure out, if I were to die in this situation, who Ed could marry who would be a good mother to our children! Finally, with a great lurch, we got free and kept going. After what seemed like hours, we reached the other side. The creek bank had washed away, and there was a nearly vertical wall to climb. The logger had some trouble getting up out of the creek and I had to hold on to my awkward perch for dear life to keep from falling into the rushing water, but eventually we made it.

The people on the other side were expecting (hoping ?) to see us, and they were delighted that we – and the generators – had made it. Under the circumstances, we were probably more welcome than Santa Claus. We unloaded the generators and other gear, bade the ranger and others farewell, and headed back down into the creek, which seemed like it was deeper and swifter than before.

We could barely see the truck lights on the far side, and after what again seemed like hours, we made it safely back to the store area where Ed and the locals were gathered. Ed had begun to worry about what was taking us so long, and he was much relieved to see the old Cat come up out of the water. I thanked the logger for getting us back safely, and he said it was no XXM## big deal, but I was welcome.

By now it was long after we had expected to be back home, but the phone lines were out, Ed's car radio wouldn't reach the F.S. mountaintop radio repeaters, so Ed couldn't talk back to the forest dispatcher in Redding, and there was nothing to do but head back to Redding. We got back after 10 P.M., retrieved our worried kids from our neighbors, and really counted our many blessings.

It had not been the Christmas Day we expected, and certainly the rough logger with the colorful vocabulary did not at all look like Santa Claus, but together, in our own ways, we had brought to those beleaguered people what must have been to them some very welcome cheer.

RANGER WIFING IN THE 60'S
by Betty Filius

People have asked me to write of my experiences living on a ranger station back in the 1960's, thinking I suppose that I'll relate something unique, interesting and exciting. My memories of that era seem much more mundane.

For example, moving to six different places in that decade gives me memories of packing and unpacking and even saving boxes. Adventures were of a U-haul nature. My Dad, a farmer, wondered why my new husband couldn't hold down a job. Twice we did that moving adventure while I was eight months pregnant and always with little kids.

We did enjoy meeting an array of new found friends. For example at my wedding shower in Helena, I only knew one person amongst the roomful of faces, all of them F.S. wives like myself who were mostly from homes far away. They included names like Hendzel, Sclamp, Evans, Mershon, Engler and Hamre; retiree names many of you still remember.

We lived at first in a upstairs apartment in Helena where we shared a bath with two other tenants. Later we moved into a small house down at the "service site" by the airport. Until we had enough fire money to afford more furniture and carpet, the bare wooden floors made that place echo like an empty gymnasium.

I recall the next little rental house in Watford City, North Dakota, a ranching and oil boom town where in the winter the frost would collect on the inside of the uninsulated kitchen wall. In the summer when I went out to hang clothes on the backyard clothesline, it would often be in a swarm of mosquitoes. Two little kids now made the daily laundry pile grow. We were there when the news from Dallas told us that John F. Kennedy had been shot. Richmond, Hensler and Byrne were kindred families we shared all that with.

In 1964, after a long trek west across Montana and then into Idaho, we settled briefly in an old-radar base housing area near Cottonwood where a third new baby arrived shortly after unpacking. I also recall that memorable day when a child's crisis distracted me while melting some canning wax. I returned to a roiling inky cloud of waxy smoke in our newly painted kitchen. The memory is in the scrubbing. The crises in Vietnam was in the news.

A few months later we repacked and moved down on the Selway River to a new and muddy Cedar Flats Job Corps Center. We lived in a almost idyllic cedar and fern shaded site by the river. My homemaker job at that point acquired the added excitement of keeping kids either out of the river in the back, or off the busy road out front. However, again less than a year later, we repacked and moved.

By this time you should get the picture that we did not yet have the convenience of movers in white who came to pack and load for us. But that chore done once again, we were off to Anaconda, Montana.

The Job Corps Center near that smelter city was still raw and newly built. We moved into a brand new house with a clear view of the snow capped Pintlar peaks. There was a new cast of young mothers and little kids to greet us. Here I was able to help teach survival swimming to corpsmen at an indoor pool in town. Another memory is of trying to bundle up three little kids to go out and play in the snow. By the time the third tyke was snowsuited and mittened, the first one was cold and wanting to come in. Job Corps added names like Nelson, Labrier, Johnson and Sherick to our list of new friends.

The final move of the decade, in 1967, was to Noxon, Montana, a ranger district on the old Kaniksu National Forest. What a beautiful setting. The station, new in 1964, included two new houses on a sloping grassy lawn beneath tall whispering white pine and larch. Here we had our fourth baby, but now the other three were tykes old enough to play more freely outside with neighbor kids. Cone gathering in the fall, and swimming and canoeing in the reservoir were fun times. This was where we were when Neil Armstrong stepped off his Eagle lander onto the moon. Familiar retiree names like Brooks, Bowles and Righter were added to our Christmas list.

These adventures were fun times for us, but it was a decade of my life focused on child rearing. This by nature included lots of repetition, sometimes cabin fever, often downright exhaustion. While Dave was out and about at his job, my job was home cooking, feeding, sewing, laundry and child tending. This might seem mundane, and perhaps the war stories of F.S. wives in that era could easily be left at that. Many women in the 60's rebelled at that role. I found it rewarding. The mostly assigned moves of that period added to the new places were able sample. The many moves gave us a long list of family-like friends to keep in touch with. This made each new move a little easier to take in stride. Our neighbors on the compounds became more than mere acquaintances, they were almost like brothers and sisters, aunts and uncles, in short – family, Forest Service family. Our children often met each other again in college.

The frequent moving had made them adaptable and confident. It also made us a closer more tightly knit family. Life was good.

We spent the 1970's at three more ranger station, but that's another story.

AS SOON AS POSSIBLE
by Nita Hearst

In May of 1965, the Job Corps was recruiting for Forest Service employees to open the various centers. Roger had not signed up. The Plains District Ranger, Dale Thacker, was one that was going to be a center director. He was home for the weekend. He called one evening – Roger was at a meeting, but he wanted to talk to him tonight. At 11 o'clock, Dale was asking Roger to come try it out. Roger said I'll let you know in the morning. Dale said, "I'm leaving at 5:30, I need to know tonight."

Roger said he'd give it a try and left the following Sunday. If he made the cut after one week, then there would be another week of training. After the first week, I got the call to put the house up for sale and start packing. We were suppose to be in Dickinson, North Dakota, ASAP. We were there the first week of June.

Our third son was born in March of that first year. He was late in coming. A blizzard arrived before he did. We were four miles out of town and there had been one trip to the hospital with false labor. In the morning the snow was on one side of the house and at night it was on the other side of the house. This went on for four days. I didn't know it at the time, but everyone was sitting on pins and needles, figuring what would have to be done in the event that he came while the storm still raged. There was a bulldozer (which wouldn't have run) and a nurse a couple houses away. He waited until the way was cleared – then he came breach.

We were at the Center for four years. The announcement that the center was closing came while Roger was in the hospital with five breaks in the femur of his left leg. He was in the hospital for two months. Who wants an employee on crutches? Dale came to the house one afternoon – Roger was in the bathtub trying to get his leg to bend. Dale went right in to discuss the matter at hand. Would he like to go to Superior? Roger could only think of the Superior National Forest in Michigan, but NO – Superior, Montana, in fire control.

Yes, he'd take the job. Roger was a great supervisor of the moving operation, as he was on crutches. We had a good four years at the Job Corps Center, but it was good to get back in western Montana.

ADVICE TO THE FORESTRY WIVE'S CLUB
AT THE UNIVERSITY OF IDAHO
IN 1966
by Ruth Kern

When the president of your club requested that I speak to you tonight about Forest Service life, and especially about the life of a ranger's wife, I couldn't help but smile to myself and add one more requirement to the long, long list of pleasurable and challenging duties. All the world is a stage, and no one realizes it more than the wife of a U.S. Forest Service Ranger. She has the opportunity to play many varied roles, depending on her personality and attitude. This opportunity to be a guest speaker is one of the most pleasurable and I sincerely thank you for the invitation.

Over the past decade, I have been called upon to play many parts. I have come to the conclusion, that because my husband works for the federal government, and because public relations is a vital segment of his job, that the townspeople feel that I, as his "relation," belong to the "public." Sometimes this is difficult to accept, and many women cannot do it. Personally, I feel that if a Ranger's wife can accept this challenge as helpmate to her husband as a public servant, it becomes a fulfilling advantage and not just another burden.

In addition to the normal roles we all play, no matter whom we marry, such as wife, mother, Sunday School teacher, PTA President, Room Mother and Little League Umpire, as Ranger's wife, I have also been a MIDWIFE, a BEAR TRAPPER, an AMBULANCE DRIVER, a DISPATCHER, a SEARCH and RESCUE worker, the GOVERNOR'S Chauffeur, a RADIO OPERATOR, a FIRECOOK'S HELPER, a FIRE SPOTTER, performed MINOR SURGERY on the kitchen table, and one time, at midnight, I scouted the local taverns, all 12 of them for emergency fire fighters, when there were no more men left on the Ranger Station.

As your young husbands step out into the future, as professional foresters, perhaps they, too, will seek an appointment with the U.S. Forest Service. Then you will discover, rather sadly, that Uncle Sam's forest becomes their first love. You and the kids fall in just after their Forest, their Gun and their Dog in that order. You will find that you have to share your husband with the Bark Beetle, Hunting Season and the Fishing Streams. You will learn to do things you thought only a man should do, when all the men on the station are fighting fire or cruising a timber sale. You will learn to live with all kinds of people and share their happiness and their sorrows. You will learn to respond to a way of life which will reap rewards in the form of security, contentment, and a satisfaction which will make your years on a ranger station the happiest years of your life. I really can't think of any forester that doesn't love his job and his way of life. It never ceases to amaze me to see such a dedicated and wholesome group of men that I have come to know in the Forest Service.

Many of you have already spent your summers on a station, where you were caught up in the whirlwind activity of fire season excitement. Truly the summers are something to write home about, but the real test of a devoted forest service wife is the ability to smile through the long cold winter months. My husband calls them "cabin fever" months. The current crop of Ranger's wives have never had it so good! It is probable that by the time your husband becomes the chief of a district, you will move into a fairly new three bedroom residence, with thermostatically controlled heat, and every electrical convenience at your finger tips. A far cry from the woman of thirty years ago who moved into a two bedroom log cabin, on the bank of a creek, which served as living quarters and also as the Ranger's office and warehouse. Conditions have greatly improved for the Forest Service wife, over the years, and even the most remote station has at least a light plant and a livable comfortable house. This type of living condition is being replaced with modern stations as quickly as government financing and the yards of red tape will allow.

We have come a long way from the days when a Ranger was fired for getting married during fire season, and from the days when women considered themselves fortunate to be there on the station with their husband. For the most part, Uncle Sam is relocating and trying to build the station on a surfaced road with easy access to town and schools. Although there are still many exceptions, great strides have been made to furnish government foresters with creature comforts.

It was my pleasant experience to observe and to "strawboss" the building of a complete new ranger station, and then when the doors were opened, to be the first woman to live there. In fact, I was one of three wives to move into the new residences, and I will never forget how excited we all were pouring over color charts and drapery samples. The Jr. Forester as we called the newcomers, had recently completed a tour of duty in the Army and he and his wife were so thrilled with their new home. They purchased a washer and dryer, a big freezer, a stereo, even an electric ice cream maker and settled back to await the arrival of their first baby. They were with us just six months more and the new baby arrived along with a promotion and a transfer. Even before she came home from the hospital, her husband had packed and started the move to a backwoods station, with a light plant that could be turned on for only a few hours a day. So with her brand new baby, she moved into a log house with a wood stove and oil and propane lanterns, and fifty miles of mountain roads to drive to the nearest town. Her brand new appliances were put in storage and she heated water on a wood stove to wash diapers. She took all this in her stride and really proved the kind of "stuff" a Forest Service Wife is made of. She has passed her first milestone in accepting the unexpected. When I marveled at her cheerfulness, I received my husband's standard reply, "she hired out to be tough!" She must have been, for they were there for four years and I never heard her gripe once. Speaking of griping, we are all guilty of it at times, especially when the subject of Hard Road versus Dirt Road philosophy arises, but, just let an outsider start to run down the Forest Service and we bristle to its defense. There is a loyal bond among us that I have never seen the likes of in any other walk of life.

I think that a healthy attitude is the greatest asset a F.S. wife can have, and the type of attitude she fosters from the very beginning can sometimes make or break her husband's career. I have seen some women make their husband's lives miserable by playing the part of a martyr who has forfeited the culture of the big metropolis. If you can't make the transition from tweeds and cashmeres to a sweat shirt and blue jeans, then you had better come to realize it before your husband makes the big decision.

You will have to learn to overcome petty jealousy, especially when others advance ahead of your husband. Every wife thinks that her husband is the best, but sometimes finds it isn't necessarily so! You have to learn to smile and say "that's the way the cookie crumbles." It's that way in any large organization, be it federal or private.

I think it's important to be considerate of the individuality of the Ranger's Rules, as long as he is reasonable. Some of the cardinal sins that wives of personnel commit, make the Ranger's blood boil! For instance, the office is not a coffee shop. Also, Rangers expect the wives to keep the government houses reasonable clean, and keep the children away from the work area. Then, too, to keep a first impression a pleasant and lasting one, families of the station complement should be courteous to tourists and visitors who might happen to find their way to the private residences. I will always remember all but one accepted the fact when told that the houses were not open for inspection. All except one red-faced town busy body who insisted that because she paid her taxes, she had the right to tramp through the house muddy feet and all. The young wife became just as red-faced and informed her that she had also paid her taxes and her rent, and furthermore a man's home is his castle and no one was going to inspect it unless personally invited to do so. Then to add insult to injury, she added that if the intruder would simply tell her the amount of her taxes, she would gladly chip off a piece of the fireplace brick and she could consider herself paid in full. Of course, this wasn't the right attitude, or the way to handle an adverse reaction from John Q. Public. There are many times when discretion is the better part of valor.

Another quality one develops, sometimes from necessity, is poise, or the art of quick recovery in regard to composure. More times than I'd like to remember, my husband would call at 5 P.M. and say "can you throw another bean in the pot?" More often than not it was the night before a 60 mile trip to town for groceries and Mother Hubbard's cupboard was bare. After times like this, you learn to keep an emergency shelf with supplies enough to fill an extra plate or two, and not to press the panic button. One thing is for sure. Even though your guest is top man on the totem pole, it is comforting to know that at one time or another, his wife has been in the very same position. I have yet to meet a forester from the Washington, D.C., office right on down to the back country packer that couldn't sit down, elbow to elbow at the kitchen table and make you think that it was the best meal they had ever eaten.

When my husband discovered that I was going to speak to you tonight his analytical mind, compounded by dedicated devotion to his work, prompted him to suggest that I should have on hand pages of boring government statistics. This brought to mind the story of the professor of mathematics and statistics. One day, he was standing in his bathing suit at the edge of the swimming pool on campus, when a beautiful coed accidently dropped her camera in the deep end of the pool. She called to the elderly professor for help. He said he would be glad to dive down after the camera, but first wanted to know why she had chosen him when there were so many young men within reach to do the job. She answered, "Professor, you have apparently forgotten me, but I am a student in your large statistics class. I have found that you can go down deeper, stay down longer, and come up drier than any one I know!" This speaker does not propose to go down too deep, stay down too long, or come up too dry, so I accidently left his government statistics at home In conclusion it appears to me that a Ranger's wife must be cheerful, courteous, thrifty, poised, healthy, uncomplain-ing, eager, versatile, dedicated, unselfish, tidy, vigorous, brave and loyal.

Boil them down, think about them. Really a Ranger's wife is no different than any other wife. Aren't these the attributes necessary to any woman dedicated to her husband and family? Ask any Forest Service wife. We'd rather fight than switch.

A VERY MEMORABLE CHRISTMAS
by Nancy Cron

Have you ever noticed how many of the most memorable events in our lives are ones that involve hardship, adversity, or what seem like bad times at the time? Christmas of 1968 was one of those times for us. Larry and I were living on the ranger district compound in Hayfork, California, 70 miles west of Redding.

I was six and a half months pregnant with our first child, and the Christmas season found me busy with holiday preparations for a visit from Larry's grandmother, parents, and brother Bob and his wife, Jane. Our in-house family, besides the two of us, included our German Shorthair, Finnegan, and his pick-of-the-liter eight week old son, Huckleberry, who was Larry's Christmas gift to his brother. Our 2 bedroom house was one of the old "B" styles that had the bathroom situated between the two bedrooms and no access off the hallway; so for privacy all the visiting family members had rooms reserved at a local motel.

The night before and the day of their arrival (12/23) brought snow, snow, and more snow; three feet of the white stuff came down like saddle blankets weighing down and breaking tree limbs and utility lines. Well, wouldn't you know it, our house and the motel were both electric baseboard heat, not to mention the cook stove and water heater. The afternoon of the twenty-third was the last electricity we were to see or feel for three days.

Larry's parents and grandmother arrived first after fighting their way through the storm from Mt. Shasta, and because of no electricity at the motel, came to our house. Bob and Jane arrived just after dark in their pickup with chains on and abandoned it stuck in the circular driveway that served our house and three others.

Needless to say, we were very thankful for the large old fashioned fireplace we had in the living room and the cord of wood Larry had stacked near our back door. Gramma Beth was appointed to sleep on the roll-a-way in the spare bedroom (soon to be nursery) to be near the bathroom. Larry and I had the back bedroom with windows on three sides and fartherest from the fireplace (brr). Larry's parents got the hide-a-bed in the toasty warm living room next to the fireplace. Jane was tucked in on Mom's side of the hide-a-bed, and Bob got the comfy sleeping quarters on the floor in the kitchen.

I had food for an army made up in the freezer, but, not knowing how long the power would be out, I was only able to get in it once a day for a "quick" pull out. Standard fare for snacks and some meals, including Christmas breakfast, consisted of some of my hamburger turnovers in a Dutch oven hung in front of the fireplace. The womenfolk kept water heated over the fireplace or on the Coleman stove for hot drinks while the men fought with nasty elements outside, i.e., shoveling, shoveling and more shoveling.

One family had a gas oven in their trailer, and we womenfolk worked out schedules for when we could run our turkeys over for cooking on Christmas day. Luckily, about half of the 10 families on the compound had gone elsewhere for the holidays. Those of us left behind got the job done in spite of the three day power outage. I don't remember when we had Christmas dinner, only that it was very good after two days of hamburger turnovers and Coleman stove cooking.

For a young bride this was quite an experience, but it has been remembered as one of the best family Christmases ever (though I have no desire to repeat it).

REMEMBERING
by Jean Hunter

Remember old friends who made my life special by their actions:

Estelle Gaffney, (Mrs. John P. Gaffney) who was an old-time ranger's wife and who had great stories to tell about their time on the Clearwater National Forest. For this newlywed on the Republic District, Colville N.F., she was a great neighbor and friend.

Dolly Holmgre, cook at Raven Ranger Station, Fisher River District, Kootenai N. F. She was not only a wonderful cook, but a good friend. She was always there to help, baked birthday cakes for our kids, lemon pies for me, shot a bear that was bothering around the station (yes, in season), and then cooked a roast for me so I would know how to cook bear meat.

Audrey Westaner, (Mrs. Dave Westaner) also at Fisher River District, was a local Libby girl. She generously shared her knowledge of the area and her family besides being fun to pal around with and a good neighbor.

Willy Terry, (Mrs. David Terry) I first met her at St. Maries, Idaho, St. Joe National Forest. She was so interesting to be around. I always learned something new and good from her. Later when she lived in Missoula and I in Hamilton, during a long evening spent in St. Patrick's Hospital, she and Dave spent the evening with me. She was that kind of person.

These ladies are gone, but I think about them often, and our time spent together.

Remembering also, Billy Damon (Mrs. Bob Damon), when we first moved to the St. Joe National Forest, St. Maries, Idaho, who brought flowers when we first moved into our house, making me feel especially welcome.

Carol Rowley, who lived next door for a short time we lived at Trapper Creek Job Corps Center, Bitterroot National Forest. It was almost like being on the district again, someone close by to coffee and visit with.

Barb Ormiston, (Mrs. John Ormiston), on the Bitterroot National Forest, who has been a good friend for more than twenty years and for almost that amount of time a Wednesday lunch partner.

My most favorite Forest Service lady is, of course, our daughter, Patty Hunter McAlpin (Mrs. Rob). Rob is the District Engineer on the Powers Ranger District, Siskiyou N. F. They live in Myrtle Point, Oregon, where Patty is thoroughly Modern Milly. She teaches in the Myrtle Point, Oregon, school system.

It's a good thing we have retirees reunions, otherwise we wouldn't get to see friends who live nearby. Retirees are the busiest people in the world.

REFLECTING ON BEING A F.S. WIFE
by Kay Bennett

Jack and I were married when Jack was thirty-eight and I was twenty-two years old, so I missed out on living in a ranger station with him when he was younger. We had twins within the first year of marriage, which increased Jack's income tax deductions from one to four in one year. Now that made him happy! He was a wonderful father to our three sons and enjoyed watching them grow up and become fine young men. By the time Jack died in January 1994, all the boys had finished up their college education and were on their own. He can be very proud of each of them. Now he has a grandson named after him.

Jack and Kay Bennett and sons Doyle, John and Dan, 1969.

What I enjoyed so much about being a F.S. wife was that when we moved to a new place, there were usually people we knew there. Jack had made friends with Al Crozer in Montana, saw him again in Alaska, and when we moved to Denver in 1968, there he was again with his wife, Kay, and four children. In Juneau we were good friends with Gene Chelstad and his wife Vivian and two children. When we moved to Virginia in 1978, Gene and his family lived just a half a mile from us in Greenbrier

Jack Bennett – 1959 Juneau, Alaska.

subdivision of Fairfax. We'd had another son and so had they since we'd all lived in Juneau, and those two boys became fast friends. Bob & Vella Sullivan lived in Denver when we moved there, and we were so fortunate to renew our friendship when we moved to Virginia. In Missoula, Jack picked up right where he left off with his friendship with Don Durland and Ray and Jane Karr. I didn't really know them before that.

One thing I always wanted to do, after Jack retired, was get all our friends together from various parts of the country, and take a cruise. That would've given all of us such a good opportunity to visit and catch up on everything! Now what I like to do is telephone friends across the country. It doesn't cost that much to talk to someone. E-mail is wonderful, but there's something about hearing someone's voice that e-mail doesn't satisfy.

My advice to everyone. Make that phone call to your friend before it's too late. Jack was so lucky to have friends who made the effort to come and see him during his last months. Many who couldn't visit in person called him. Thank you all!

THE LIFE FOR A WIFE
RANGER STATION LIVING
by Betty Filius

It was February, 1970, at the Noxon Ranger Station in Noxon, Montana, and the snow was nearly up to the eaves. I was snowbound in a three bedroom ranger station house with four children, 8, 5, 4, and 2, and we were starting to pack for a move to the Slate Creek Ranger District on the Nezperce National Forest in Idaho.

Outside, Ike Rasmussen, from the Enco gas station across the river, was hunched over the levers of his little yellow bulldozer trying valiantly to push away the wet snow so we could get a moving van up to the house. The snow piles he made formed walls that we couldn't see over as we drove in and out with our '68 Rambler station wagon.

The district employees invited us to a going-away dinner at the Hereford Supper Club, and our friends at the little circuit-rider Methodist Church gave us a nice framed print called "Grace" that still hangs in our home to this day. Almost every night that last week we were invited out to eat at someone else's home.

Besides almost full-time nose wiping, diaper changing, clothes washing, picking up toys and general housekeeping, we did have an enjoyable wives group of young mothers like myself. Likewise, we visited frequently back and forth with other Forest Service families and other young families, particularly school teachers and some young families at the nearby Noxon Rapids Dam.

In the winter, the main social gathering places were either the high school gym for basketball games, the church for Sunday services, the three local bars for the after work or out of work crowd, or Mac and Marion McKee's grocery store and the post office.

Betty and Dave Filius and kids – 1968. Noxon Ranger Station Kaniksu National Forest.

Usually, I just bundled up the three youngest and we walked and pulled a sled to the store, since it was only a block or two from the station. For major grocery purchases we hitched up a two wheel trailer with a plywood box and headed to Spokane where we loaded up at a food warehouse. Believe it or not, we could fill that 4' x 8' x 2' box with groceries for about $150.00.

The move to Slate Creek was like moving to Arizona. When we left the cavernous snow piles of Noxon it was like the dead of winter. We arrived at Slate Creek and the weather was shirt sleeve and the grass was greening up. Kids were out playing on the lawn.

At Slate Creek there were three houses, three trailers, and a duplex in progress, the latter, compliments of the Job Corps. Two of the neighbors were bachelor foresters, but the others were all families with kids the age of ours, a mix of preschoolers and grade schoolers.

Since Grangeville was up over the multi-switchbacked White Bird Hill, and little Riggins was twenty miles or so down canyon, I busied myself mainly around the house, yard and garden.

We raised almost every sort of vegetable, had lots of locally grown fruit, and spent long hot summer afternoons at the nearby sandy roadside beaches along the Salmon River. The kids camped out with neighbor friends in the back yard and when we weren't at the beach they played ball on the huge lawn or splashed in a small portable swimming pool.

Communication in and out of Slate Creek in any direction was long distance, but each house on the station had a wall mounted crank telephone for talking back and forth. Each house had a special sequence of long and short rings.

Summer fire busts were all hands events at Slate Creek. The district fire crew was kept busy chasing lightning fires up and down the steep Salmon River and Snake River Canyons. Often, we wives and kids would drive up the road so we could watch the crews in the orange and yellow shirts as they scratched fire line on the steep slopes. Occasionally, we were lucky enough to see an air drop of retardant flown in from Grangeville. On one particular fire bust, the wives were called on by the hot short crew cooks to help prepare sack lunches for several smoke chaser crews. When we ran out of lunch meat, we were forced to slap together some peanut butter and cheese sandwiches. I can imagine the water it took to get those down!

In the summer the station hosted a regional hot shot fire crew and

Snow removal at Noxon Ranger Station, February 1969.

one of the evening highlights was when some of the wives and husbands would play volley ball with the crew members. These were fun and spirited games, and by the end of the summer we knew all the boys by name, and could spike a pretty good volleyball too.

Our life at Slate Creek was quite peaceful and sheltered. In the outside world, the horrors of Vietnam and the problems of Watergate seemed to blather on over our heads and we lived out our lives in a canyon with almost no radio and very little tv.

During a twelve year period, we lived on three ranger station compounds and in one small ranger station community, and although life has always been good to us, the life experiences and friendships of those ranger station days still have a comfortable grip on us.

Back then, most of the wives were working at home and the Forest Service was still an almost all male organization. Life today on a ranger station compound may be much the same, or perhaps much different, I don't know. I hear some of them have been bombed and others are surrounded by chain link fence. Many are closed, or no longer have families living at them. But for us, in the late 60's and 70's, ranger station living was a good way to raise a family.

POWELL RANGER STATION: THE FIRST NIGHT
by Nancy Cron

Larry and I arrived at Powell R.S. on January 20, 1972. Just getting there coming from the west was an achievement because Highway 12 had been closed for two weeks in early January with numerous avalanches, one which severely damaged the Eagle Mountain pack bridge. A cold spell had set in, and though the sky was clear, blue and sunny, at two o'clock in the afternoon at Powell it was 20 below zero. It was so cold, in fact, that we had difficulty sleeping in our bed that night because our mattress was so cold and, along with everything else coming out of the moving van, seemed to be frozen solid.

I remember walking through the F.S. residence looking for the telephone so that I could call my folks to tell them that we'd arrived safely, only to find NO PHONE. We finally found a crank wall phone in the hall closet but that was only for calling a few other residences, the office and several lookouts. There was no telephone to the outside world. The next day we found out that the only outside communication was a radio-phone in the office.

Having worked in payroll in the Plumas N.F. Supervisor's Office and using the radio only when absolutely necessary, the prospect of communicating with friends and family by radio-phone was not something I looked forward to doing again. Letter writing, for me became the favored method of communication.

The wives at Powell at that time were certainly hardier and more adaptable than I was prepared to be, for they had endured with only the station generators for electricity up until the summer before our arrival when the underground powerline from Lolo Hot Springs was completed over Lolo Pass. Yikes! This was really an outback place even for a hill-people California girl like me to imagine.

The highlights of our time at Powell, for me, were the friendships and closeness we share with others living on the ranger station compound, and at the Lochsa Lodge and highway maintenance station. The birth of our second daughter, Theresa, and raising our children in a safe environment where there was lots of time to give them was certainly a plus. Our oldest daughter, Michelle, attended first grade in the brand new one room school house that I could see from our front window. The highlight of each spring and talk of the station was when the mules arrived from their winter pasture in the low country and though the calendar said

Ranger's dwelling at Powell Ranger Station – 1972.

it was late May or early June, we finally knew that winter was over and summer not far behind. Everyone watched anxiously and then gathered at the corral when they finally arrived. With the short summer season would come picnics at Powell campground, at Packer Meadows in all its glory covered with blue camas flowers, and at Elk Summit with snow cones on the 4th of July and elk, deer, and/or moose at the packer's camp salt lick. With the fall rains (starting in late August) would come the gathering of shaggy mane mushrooms on the back roads.

And when the summer crews left, it would be time to stock up on good books and another six months of snow with the gentle sound of the Lochsa River flowing behind our home in the wilderness.

Powell Ranger Station cook house and mule string.

AN ALASKAN SKATING PARTY
by Fern Coutant

When our family of five moved to Anchorage, Alaska, in 1975, we knew our "stint" or time to live there would not be long. Jerry was to be a part of the Alaskan Planning Team, working on the Alaskan Native Claims Settlement Act. Another member of that team, and our next door neighbor, Sig and his wife, Esther, Olson, were avid Alaskans in every way. Esther said to me "daylight hours are limited this month, get outside every minute you can. Don't let household tasks bog you down, hike, ski, walk and just play as much as you can." This philosophy permeated our two years in the 49th state, and in retrospect, I'm so grateful to her for her advice.

The Forest Service Planning Team was a closely knit group and, of course, preferred to do all things out of doors regardless of the temperature or weather conditions. Thus the very first weekend we were in our home, a phone call came saying "get out your longies," "at least two pair of socks per person," "find the skate box," "and don't bother bringing food," "we're having a skating picnic!" My resistance to such a proposal only got me nowhere. So the process of unearthing of each box, searching for what could possible be layered on each child began. The boxes were stacked high, the children were still flipping light switches to see which one gave them the desired result, and arguments reigned over which room needed painting first. But eventually off we went.

That month was October and it was brilliantly sunny, clear and pristine. We joined about 10 others, some of whom already had a bonfire crackling, while others were striding around the lake trying to avoid protruding limbs and overhanging boughs. The kids were more than striding, they were zipping around, yelling and chasing any moving object who responded. Throwing snow balls ?????? No, nary a one, for you see, there was no snow! It was so cold that the lake had frozen solidly, clear to the bottom, without a flake of snow surrounding it. As I gazed downward in disbelief, I could see every stem of vegetation and each piece of sedge grass standing tall as if caught off guard. Even the twigs were caught askew, poised in motionless beauty. Each was frozen solidly, locked in a upright position, looking as if it was most unexpected. The bottom muck was undisturbed – and just waiting! It was an awesome sight for us mainlanders to feel such permeating below zero temperatures and not experience snow to accompany it. We were staring into a motionless glass bowl.

It didn't take long for everyone to find themselves around the camp fire where we were handed a two pronged fork. The two prongs were able to secure our sandwich much more then a single one. Yes, we had hot, toasted sandwiches that melted in our mouths! What else we ate that beautiful day, I do not remember, but the idea of a "do it yourself hot sandwich on a cold, cold day" caught my fancy, and I'll never forget the ingenuity of it all.

After some "warmer-up-foot-rubbings," the kids were off for another round of chasings and a few hard tumbles too. The elders, with their reddened cheeks and wobbly ankles, sipped their Thermos bottle coffee and discussed "the most profound of Forest Service issues."

October only gave about five or six hours of daylight, so our skating picnic was soon abbreviated, but those wonderful welcoming people, like the Coster, Olson, Grahams, Steiger, etc. set the stage for what were two years of anticipatory surprises and joys!!

BLAME IT ON THE CAMERA
by Fern Coutant

Being with the Alaskan Planning Team in 1975, Jerry traveled a lot and had the opportunity to see a lot of its beauty. Because of his intense feeling and respect for this great land, he would come home to us and repeat "you've got to see this" or "we've got to go there." He wanted to share his inexpressible feelings and the love of this land with all. Bearing this philosophy of "make the most of every day as we will not be living in Alaska very long," our family took advantage of every day Jerry was not working.

So one Saturday we five traveled south to Johnson's Pass from Anchorage for a day of cross country skiing and picnicking. The day was perfect, the snow was fresh and all roads were open. This is not a spur of the moment occasion, but rather it had been planned and discussed for at least two weeks making the anticipation keen and the spirits high. You see, it was not easy to keep three growing bodies in the proper sizes for each sport or activity. Each must have three kinds of boots; warm, warm snow boots, high-top water proof "break-up" boots, and wear to school type that you pull on over your shoes. Then for skiing one needed cross country boots with clamping soles and poles of the right length, downhill boots and poles and gender related warm underwear and snowsuits and mitts. Ice skates could be limited to one pair, figure skates for the girls and rough and tumble hockey skates for the boys. Friends and neighbors were great about exchanging outgrown hand-me-downs along with our frequent trips to the second hand stores.

Once we were all outfitted and backpacks loaded, we were off. In addition each person outwardly wore bells and unabashedly let them ring, plus an orange whistle inside ones clothing for emergencies. Matches for our camp fire were to be kept dry in anticipation of a hot lunch, and high carbo snacks and trail mix goodies were readily available. Once ready to go we lined up at the top of the pass for pictures, separately and together for "before and after shots." This was to be a great dream come true – skiing in Alaska as family on a gorgeous day.

The snowy terrain was not difficult even for little people 12, 9, and 7 years of age, but the difficulty we came to find out was to keep everyone warm at a pace all could endure. Thus Derek, at 12, wanted to go twice as fast as his little sisters and big Dad was constantly standing around monitoring both the equipment and the scenery. It was twenty minutes into this scene when Jerry realized he had set his camera on the hood of the car to adjust his bindings – and it was still there! What should we do? Should all go back and remain a unit? Should we forget the camera and consider it a frozen loss? Or should we four move on and Jerry would go back alone and then catch up to us? He was an experienced skier and could move five times as fast as we. We all agreed he would go back alone and we could take our time and enjoy our surroundings. At that point we parted company with Dad – with our dreams. It was then that the day was no longer held in eager anticipation, but had turned into an adventuresome nightmare.

The formerly cheery conversation gradually became more like grumbles and complaints "my feet are cold," "my bindings are lose," "I'm hungry," "how much further do we have to go?" "When will Dad be back?" Jerry had the biggest backpack, thus most of the food and cooking equipment, outside of our high energy food. It must have been two hours later, and admittedly three brave souls were all in tears. "What had happened to Dad?" "What should we do now?" "Will our feet and toes be frozen and have to be amputated?" "We can't walk out of here as the snow was too deep for short legs, so we'd have to put our skis back on and ski out." Those three were getting tired of "you can do it," "just a little bit more," "move those cold fingers to help with the circulation," "look all around you and enjoy the scenery" and "just wait for Dad and we'll all have a hot lunch together." They had enough encouragement from me and inwardly, too, I was genuinely worried. "Where is he?" "What was taking so long?" The wind was beginning to breathe through the trees and the snowy branches were beginning to lose their moist, heavy loads on us as we took an awaiting break. Finally, I expressed my concern to them and asked for suggestions. One said we should mark our trail, one said yell and holler all the time, and the other said blow our whistles and ring our bells. We all agreed to do all these things together; such a cacophony of sound you never have heard. It must have been this chaos that eventually caught Jerry's attention as he frantically skied and searched, faster and faster. It was getting later and later, and he could feel our apprehension. "Where are those tracks?" "Why can't I find any trace of four people?" "Did they lose the trail?" "Am I in the wrong area?" Little did either of us realize or anticipate that a breeze blowing across the top of the mountain, would whip up that beautiful, unmarred snow and fill in behind us so naturally and unconcerned. There was no trace remaining for him to follow. Determined to find us before dark, he analyzed as he sped along "what could have gone wrong?" His apprehension drove him faster and faster and he circled and searched, whistled and yelled.

Eventually our prayers were answered and along came Dad!! His clothes were wet from perspiration, his face was red from the elements beating on him, and his eyes snapped from fear, relief, and a little bit of anger.

The next moment all five of us were clasped in one big embrace with tears flowing freely. All the hopeful, yet false pretenses were cast aside, and the real fright and hopelessness was let loose. What was meant to be a twenty minute retrieval of a camera turned out to be a frightful and life-threatening ordeal.

We all sat down under a tree to analyze where we had gone wrong and how to take care of our existing misery. A fire would be the perfect solution for warming feet and fingers and toasting sandwiches. But a fire built under a tree was in itself an error, as the heat from the smoke melted the ladened boughs, bringing down moisture to blanket every flame. The good idea of hot food was soon put aside and all food was eaten "as is." Even that tasted good and we gave heartfelt thanks to God for life, limb and being together. Whatever happened to those pictures? I don't remember ever seeing them.

IT'S A SMALL WORLD
by Ruth Freeman

It was after our NRMRA (Northern Rocky Mountain Retirees Association) summer picnic in 1997 at Fort Missoula that Rocky Thompson and I were talking in the parking lot, while our husbands moved picnic tables. One's conversations seemed to revert back to "what have you been doing?" or "what are you going to do?" I mentioned how all our kids had been home for Christmas, a house full of 24 bodies! Rocky said that they were going to Wisconsin to visit her mother and sister. The next logical question, "where in Wisconsin." (I had grown up in Wisconsin) Rocky said that her Dad had been a store manager at Montgomery Wards, and they moved around a lot. I mentioned how as a kid a family with two girls moved in across the street from us whose Dad was a manager at Montgomery Wards. Rocky asked if I remembered their names? I really had to think – "I don't remember the last name, but I think the girls' names were Roxana and Lorraine." "That's me, and my sister!" Rocky exclaimed.

Jim and I have visited with Rocky and Vern since we moved back to Montana. Never questioned why she was called Rocky. Just thought it was a nickname, and we all called her that. I had lived in Two Rivers, Wisconsin, until I went away to school. But Rocky only lived there for a few years during her grade school years. Although Rocky was a year younger then I was, we were still good friends and had a mutual friend who lived in the next block. It was my first experience in making a friend and then having that friend move away. Something we have all become familiar with during our Forest Service careers. It is particularly nice to be able to find a grade school friend sixty years later, and learn she is part of your F.S. family! Rocky and I had a lot of catching up to do.

Talk about a small world!